W9-BMI-142

CANADA'S SEARCH FOR NEW ROLES

The Royal Institute of International Affairs is an unofficial body which promotes the scientific study of international questions and does not express opinions of its own. The opinions expressed in this publication are the responsibility of the author.

The Institute gratefully acknowledges the comments and suggestions of the following who read the manuscript on behalf of the Research Committee: the Hon. Alastair Buchan, John Holmes, and Professor R. T. McKenzie.

CANADA'S SEARCH FOR NEW ROLES
Foreign Policy in the Trudeau Era

Peter C. Dobell

Published for
THE ROYAL INSTITUTE OF
INTERNATIONAL AFFAIRS
by
OXFORD UNIVERSITY PRESS
LONDON   NEW YORK   TORONTO
1972

Oxford University Press

LONDON OXFORD NEW YORK

GLASGOW TORONTO MELBOURNE WELLINGTON

CAPE TOWN SALISBURY IBADAN NAIROBI DAR ES SALAAM LUSAKA ADDIS ABABA

DELHI BOMBAY CALCUTTA MADRAS KARACHI LAHORE DACCA

KUALA LUMPER SINGAPORE HONG KONG TOKYO

ISBN 0 19 285057 1

First published as an Oxford University Press paperback 1972

Set in Great Britain by
The Eastern Press Limited, London and Reading
and printed in Canada by
Web Offset Publications Limited

FOREWORD

IN a very real sense this is a collective work. I have drawn heavily on the work of the Parliamentary Centre for Foreign Affairs and Foreign Trade which has been assisting Members of Parliament of both Houses since its foundation in 1968. This is reflected in particular in the many citations from reports of the Standing Committees concerned with foreign affairs and defence of the House of Commons and Senate of the Canadian Parliament, as well as to evidence given before these Committees. I wish, however, to express my gratitude to Mrs Carol Seaborn of the Centre's staff, who has undertaken the considerable research incorporated in this slim volume. I have also immeasurably benefited from the comments of many friends who have been kind enough to read all or part of the text in manuscript, and to them I express my warm thanks.

As this book has been written primarily for readers in Britain, I have included background information where this has seemed necessary in order to make contemporary Canadian policy comprehensible to non-Canadian readers. But the approach is in no sense historical and the past has only been introduced to explain the present.

Ottawa
December 1971   P.C.D.

CONTENTS

CANADA'S POWER AND ROLE IN THE WORLD

A NATION's influence in the world is a product not only of its objective power, but also of its own and others' perceptions of it.

Canada and the United States emerged from World War II as the only two allied countries whose economies had actually been enormously strengthened. All the other major industrial and military powers, allies and enemies alike, were exhausted, if not prostrate. Canada was thus in a position to act as a minor great power. It could offer the United Kingdom a loan of $1,1250 million in 1946. In 1952, in providing twelve squadrons of fighter aircraft, Canada contributed the single largest and most advanced component of European air defence. At the same time it supplied surplus military equipment sufficient to outfit two European divisions. This power base, supported by skilful diplomacy, enabled Canada to become an important international force, as its significant role in the development of the North Atlantic Treaty showed.

Within the UN Canada played an equally central role. Limited initially to the victors, with very little representation from the Third World and with the Soviet bloc pursuing negative and destructive policies, the UN offered a natural and congenial forum in which Canada easily became a leader of the moderate and progressive nations. Newly independent nations were often content to follow a Canadian lead. Canada organized the battle which was won in 1955 for the admission of sixteen new states—and in so doing set the UN on the path to becoming a genuinely world organization. In 1948 Lester Pearson, then under-secretary of state for external affairs, chaired the First (Political) Committee of the General Assembly during the critical special session on Palestine, and it was he who was largely responsible for the setting up of the UN Emergency Force (UNEF) in 1956, thus opening up new perspectives for the UN in the field of peace keeping. Indeed, when Pearson was awarded the Nobel Prize for Peace in 1957, many felt this was a tribute not only to the man but to the Canadian foreign service and even to the country in general.

The unusual postwar situation led many Canadians to believe that Canada had become a new archetype of international politics—the middle power.

Under the impact of war, Canada has moved up from her old status to a new stature. With her smaller population and lack of colonial possessions, she is not a major or world power like Britain, the United States or Russia. But with her natural wealth and human capacity she is not a minor one like Mexico or Sweden. She stands in between as a Britannic Power of medium rank. Henceforth in world politics, Canada must figure as a Middle Power.[1]

For twenty years after World War II Canada remained a *wunderkind* in the international world, leading *The Economist* to comment on 1 July 1967:

In present conditions what is remarkable about Canada's international role is that it can be played at all. What if Canada was to withdraw from the international arena, absorbing itself in solving the still massive internal problem of its two cultures, grousing about its economic dependence on the United States, but giving up the attempt to run a foreign policy of its own? The loss would not be Canada's alone. The community of nations has learned that it needs an active Canada: as an intermediary in Commonwealth disputes, and in wider ones that range ex-imperial powers against former dependencies; as a factor that moderates the disproportion between American and European strengths in the Atlantic world; as a dispassionate but not apathetic participant in projects that are based on a tenuous international consensus (p. 13).

By 1967, however, the international picture had changed. Canada had long ceased to be the second principal Western power. The admission of large numbers of recently independent states, combined with the adoption of a more flexible approach by the nations of the Soviet bloc, had radicalized UN politics. Canada no longer found it possible to be in the vanguard on most colonial questions. More important, peacekeeping, the star in Canada's UN diadem, no longer shone with the same

[1] Lionel Gelber, *A Greater Canada among the Nations.* (Behind the Headlines ser., Toronto, 1944), p. 10.

brilliance. Canada was still active in the UN, but the organization no longer offered Canada opportunities for significant international achievements.

So, too, in the larger international arena. The United States and the USSR were, more than ever, in a class by themselves as international rivals. Great nations laid low in World War II had recovered in power and purpose—France, Germany, Japan, and China. New nations of considerable regional significance had acquired the necessary confidence to follow their national interests, India and Indonesia being the most important. In relative terms, Canada was now in a different class.

The changes in international power have, of course, been only relative. Canada's economy and population have continued to grow rapidly in the postwar years. Only its military forces have been reduced from the peak reached after the Korean war, but those remaining are of high professional competence. Canada is still, therefore, a nation of considerable *potential* force, still within the ' top ten ' on the basis of most of the usual indices.

The government of Pierre-Elliott Trudeau decided to take into account the new situation in which Canada found itself. In his first major foreign policy statement, the new prime minister offered Canadians the following appreciation of their international standing:

Re-assessment has become necessary not because of the inadequacies of the past but because of the changing nature of Canada and the world around us. . . . Canada's position in the world is now very different from that of the post-war years. Then we were probably the largest of the small powers. Our currency was one of the strongest. We were the fourth or fifth trading nation and our economy was much stronger than the European economies. We had one of the very strongest navy and air forces. But now Europe has regained its strength. The Third World has emerged.[2]

Trudeau went on to promise, if his government were returned in the June election, to undertake a major review of foreign policy.

In this situation of apparent decline in influence, the nation's image of itself is of great significance. Most Canadians probably

[2] Office of the PM, press release, 29 May 1968.

still regard their country as a middle power. The threefold concept of international ranking had been deliberately advanced by the prime minister, Mackenzie King, as World War II was coming to an end. In adding an intermediate layer of middle powers between great and small powers, King was seeking to increase Canada's internationally recognized standing abroad, as well as building up the image Canadians had of themselves. The attempt was successful to the point where it became and remains the commonly accepted way in Canada of looking at the world. But Canadians must ponder an important question: does ' middle power ' have significance in the abstract, divorced from geography and other relevant influences? Is it enough merely to grade nations according to relative economic and military power? And, to raise yet another consideration, do internal factors have a significance?

Herman Kahn, lecturing to a military audience in Ottawa in 1968, advanced the proposition that the world is divided into great, regional (as distinct from *middle*), and smaller powers. He then accounted for Canada's recent international decline with an aphorism to the effect that Canada is a regional power without a region, meaning, of course, that the natural zone of Canadian influence is pre-empted by the United States. From this perspective, Canada's remarkable effectiveness internationally in the first postwar decade resulted, not because it was the strongest of the middle powers (as Mackenzie King used to say) but because for a brief period, it was able to behave as a minor great power—free, able, and ready to operate on the world stage. Once this was no longer so, Canada became and remains a power like India or France, primarily capable of regional influence. Unlike these and other nations, however, Canada has no natural glacis for the exercise of its power locally or, by extension, in former colonial territories.

Trudeau's first foreign-policy statement, which took account of Canada's relatively diminished international power, also revealed the important additional point that he had reverted to the pre-Mackenzie King twofold division of the world. In talking of the postwar era, he referred to Canada as ' probably the largest of the *small powers* ' (italics added). Was this description carefully chosen or spontaneous? In either event it is surely a significant indication of the way Trudeau looks at the world, consistent with an observation made exactly three years later to a journalist who accompanied him to Moscow that ' we have discarded the view that Canada should try to react to all international events and have a policy on everything that happened in the world '.[3]

Since perception influences aspiration, this view of Canada as a small power will have its implications for Canada's international role while Trudeau remains prime minister. Objectively, however, does it make much difference whether Canada is seen as a small power or as a regional power without a region ? What is important when means are limited is that objectives are carefully selected. Here the Trudeau government does appear to be asking the right questions. ' We shall do more good by doing well what we *know* to be within our resources to do than to pretend either to ourselves or to others that we can do things clearly beyond our national capacity.'[4]

The Trudeau administration's foreign-policy review

With the announcement on 3 April 1969 that ' the Canadian government intends, in consultation with Canada's allies, to take early steps to bring about a planned and phased reduction of the size of the Canadian forces in Europe ',[5] the first move in a major shift seemed to be in the making. Denis Healey's outburst at the NATO Defence Planning Committee in May 1969 (when he was minister of defence)—' Canada [is] passing the buck to the rest of us '[6]—was a public expression of a reaction widely shared by Europeans. Undoubtedly the intensity of these feelings resulted mainly from a fear that Canada's decision to reduce its forces would encourage a comparable United States withdrawal and stimulate pressures for force reductions in their own countries. That this has not happened, that Canadian force reductions were actually less than feared and carried out in close consultation with the NATO authorities, and that the remaining forces are to be retained in Europe, have ended the immediate state of alarm felt by Europeans about Canadian

[3] Press interview with radio reporters en route from Soviet tour, 28 May 1971.
[4] Office of the PM, press release, 29 May 1968.
[5] Office of the PM, press release.
[6] *The Times*, 29 May 1969.

intentions. A more balanced and perhaps more realistic assessment of Canada's interest in Europe now prevails.

But if abroad Canada did not lose its reputation as an internationally-minded state—albeit one with difficult internal problems—many Canadians were more deeply shaken. Peyton Lyon expressed this concern in more forceful terms than most:

We are retreating from Europe, failing to increase our activity in other areas or organizations to any significant degree and taking a giant step in the direction of continental isolationism. If not quite a free ride in world affairs, we are taking one that will be much cheaper, and more sharply focused on national interests.[7]

The completion of the government's promised review of important areas of foreign policy helped considerably to allay fears about its intentions. *Foreign Policy for Canadians*, issued by the Department of External Affairs, was submitted to parliament on 25 June 1970, in six separate booklets in a box container: a master booklet bearing the title, and five subordinate booklets entitled *Latin America*, *Pacific*, *Europe*, *United Nations*, and *International Development*. But the policy papers have not overcome all doubts. Concern has been expressed in particular over the inference that past policy had a 'reactive rather than active concern with world events', and the suggestion that foreign policy should and would in future be 'the extension abroad of national policies'.[8] This apparent rejection of the achievements of the postwar years, a source of pride to many Canadians, when seen alongside direct, unveiled statements that foreign policy was to be the projection of national policies abroad, inevitably gave rise to concern within the country that Canadian policy was to be significantly reoriented and was in future to be more self-serving. However unjustified the concern, it was widespread. It has revealed itself in particular in some of the testimony before the House of Commons Standing Committee on External Affairs and National Defence which conducted hearings from November 1970 to June 1971 on the first general booklet of *Foreign Policy for Canadians* and is reflected in a more balanced form in the Committee's report.[9]

[7] 'A Review of a Review', *J. Canadian Stud.*, May 1970, p. 34.
[8] *Foreign Policy for Canadians* (*FPC*), pp. 8, 9.
[9] Parliament, H. of C. Standing Committee on External Affairs and National Defence (SCEAND), *4th Report*, June 1971.

Yet the impulse which led the prime minister to order the foreign-policy review resulted from the widely held doubts of many Canadians with a variety of outlooks about the country's role in the world. The policy review explicitly justified its own need on the ground that ' at times in the past, public disenchantment with Canada's foreign policy was produced in part by an over-emphasis on role and influence obscuring policy objectives and actual interests (p. 8) '. Symptomatic of this condition has been the series of polemical comments on Canadian foreign policy, representative of more radical opinion, which have spewed from the presses in the last five years: *An Independent Foreign Policy for Canada?* (1968); *Alliances and Illusions* (1969); *Silent Surrender* (1970); *Partner to Behemoth: the military policy of a satellite Canada* (1970); *Close the 49th Parallel etc., the Americanization of Canada* (1970); and *The Star-Spangled Beaver* (1971).[10] Many of these books question the traditional policies of participation in the NATO alliance and of military co-operation with the United States. They attribute these involvements and other policies to which they object to Canada's economic dependence on the United States, which they regard as the primary problem of Canadian foreign policy. In their eyes the government is guilty either of ignoring the problem or of pursuing policies which aggravate Canada's difficulties.

As Canada is a relative newcomer on the world stage, it is natural that little has been written on Canadian foreign policy in the past. Postwar writings on the subject were infrequent and uncritical, indicative of minimal public interest and what amounted to a tacit consensus on all major issues. With the ending of the era of spectacular successes, which more or less coincided with the defeat of the Liberal government in 1957, the problems of Canadian foreign policy began to grow and criticism to develop. This reflected in the main increasing public concern over Canada's relationship with the United States. But for a decade the old formulas were repeated and vigorous efforts were made to conjure up foreign policy initiatives which could produce international recognition and domestic satisfaction. It is to the credit of the Trudeau government that it publicly

[10] Respectively by Stephen Clarkson, ed., Lewis Hertzman and others, Kari Levitt, J. W. Warnock, Ian Lumsden, ed., and John Redekop, ed.

acknowledges that conditions have changed and that a new approach is needed. Its decision has been to attempt a new definition of the national interest and to tailor Canada's international effort to it.

In the process they may have overcompensated, by giving greater importance than had been admitted in the past to the conscious promotion of economic growth. But this emphasis reflects some harsh domestic and international facts. Canada has in the last few years been suffering from one of the highest levels of unemployment of any industrialized country (5·1 per cent average over the last three years, reaching as high as 8 per cent in February of 1971). The problem is aggravated because the labour force between 1965–80 is projected to grow by 49·8 per cent, a rate substantially greater than in any other developed country.[11] Because of an extraordinary dependence on foreign trade, Canada is less able than most countries to cope with economic problems through domestic action. Twenty per cent of Canada's GNP depends on exports, while the figure for Canada's neighbour to the south is only 5 per cent.

In contrast with these important international trading interests, Canada has no overriding security preoccupations on which it must concentrate its efforts. Nor can ' Canadian efforts . . . greatly affect the conditions of Canadian military security '. For these reasons, Dr Robert Osgood, an American writer on NATO questions appearing before the Commons Committee on External Affairs, asserted that ' you are freer to pursue self-interested goals other than security, especially your own economic welfare, and you are bound to pay great attention to your own interest in maintaining internal cohesion '.

Professor Osgood has accurately assessed the importance which Canadians must pay to internal unity—a perennial Canadian problem which is in a particularly acute phase at this time. From the same lack of ' compelling imperatives of security ', he also found it natural for Canadians to consider that

the United States may in some sense threaten the independence of Canada, but not [its] security and so it does not really serve the same

[11] OECD, *Demographic Trends 1965–80 in Western Europe and North America* (quoted in *Financial Times*, 12 July 1971).

function of clarifying, of organizing, of ordering policy concerns as the Soviet Union serves for the United States. The American threat, if you can call it that in quotation marks, is rather subtle and diffuse, and mixed with a lot of benefit.[12]

Dr Osgood is again correct. Proximity to the United States, while providing security in the strategic sense, is deeply troubling economically, culturally, and ultimately, politically. These considerations affect the framework within which Canadian foreign policy—and in many instances domestic policy—must be formulated and presented. They distort policy goals, too, because it is often difficult to sell policies domestically where United States and Canadian interests may coincide. It was easier, for example, for the Canadian government to support the creation of NATO because the United States was a reluctant and uncertain advocate. Canada was clearly in the vanguard. Now that the US government is a primary defender of the alliance, Canadian support is inevitably seen within the country as a pale reflection of US policy and as such comes under attack. John Holmes, Director-General of the Canadian Institute of International Affairs, has illuminated the difficulty with sardonic wit: ' To act after the Americans have done so is a kind of humiliation Canadians seek to avoid '.[13]

Since the battle of the Plains of Abraham in 1759, Canada has been swept periodically by waves of concern about its survival as a unified and independent country. At times the possibility of internal break-up has threatened the fragile ship of state; at others the danger of submersion in the wake of the United States. Today many Canadians believe that these threats have converged. It is therefore much more than mere rhetoric when the government firmly asserts, in *Foreign Policy for Canadians*, that the first aim of national policy must be ' that Canada will continue secure as an independent political entity ' (p. 10).

[12] H. of C. SCEAND, *Mins. of Proc. & Evidence*, 24 Feb. 1971.
[13] ' Canadian foreign policy ', *The World Today*, Oct. 1969, p. 457.

2

PERSONALITIES AND NEW WAYS OF CONDUCTING GOVERNMENT BUSINESS

ONE of Trudeau's first acts as leader of the Liberal party was to commit the government, if returned in the 1968 election, to a major review of foreign policy. His statement conveyed the impression that significant changes were in the wind. Many expectations aroused by this undertaking have not been satisfied; there have in practice been few major shifts of policy. But the style of government has changed greatly and in order to accentuate the differences with the past, Trudeau has elaborated a philosophical basis for Canadian policy. This rhetoric is unusually direct and candid, which may have contributed to some of the misunderstanding and concern about the future direction of Canadian foreign policy.

Trudeau is the first postwar Canadian prime minister whose outlook has not been formed by World War II. His predecessors —St Laurent, Diefenbaker, and Pearson—all believed without reservation in collective security and the Atlantic alliance and never questioned the underlying principles. Trudeau is a French Canadian who, for reasons which had widespread support in Quebec, did not serve the government in a military or civilian capacity during the war. His instinctive scepticism about military solutions found natural support among his political associates of the postwar years, many of whom were socialists. He travelled widely after the war, but, having no official position, his approach was that of an observer.

Elected to parliament for the first time in 1965, his two and a half years of experience before he was prime minister probably strengthened his scepticism. As a delegate to the UN General Assembly in 1966, Trudeau appears to have been impressed principally by the inefficacy of the organization and shocked by the contrast between the reality he observed and the image then current in Canada of the country's exaggerated influence within the UN. He saw how this image was nurtured by initiatives often of a purely procedural character, undertaken to satisfy public pressure for an active foreign policy.

Within the cabinet, which he joined as minister of justice in 1967, there appears to have been only routine, rather formal consideration of foreign policy questions. The secretary of state for external affairs, Paul Martin, believed in settling all contentious questions of policy privately with the prime minister before bringing them to the cabinet for formal decision. Though undoubtedly speedy, this technique precluded informed discussion in the cabinet. The only substantive foreign and defence policy question to be seriously examined in the cabinet during Trudeau's period as minister was the renewal of the air defence agreement (NORAD) with the United States. This experience may have been significant. It is certainly striking that, while the Trudeau government has reduced Canadian forces in Europe by 50 per cent, it has made no significant cuts in the forces contributed to NORAD. This difference in approach is the more noteworthy because most critics of Canadian foreign and defence policy have reserved their strongest attacks for this agreement.

In any event, Trudeau and some of his closest and most powerful ministerial associates, such as Jean Marchand, Gérard Pelletier, and Donald Macdonald,[1] shared, when they came into office, an evident dissatisfaction and even frustration with the foreign policy of the Pearson government. Yet only three years later, after an exhaustive review which established foreign and defence policies having many parallels with those pursued by the earlier government, their mood when they took office appeared incongruous. For Trudeau and Marchand their experience—or rather lack of experience—in the cabinet is an important key to their attitude. Although neither Pelletier nor Macdonald had previously held ministerial office, both had served—they would say suffered—as parliamentary secretaries to the secretary of state for external affairs. This experience generated in both men a deeply felt desire for change from what

[1] Marchand and Pelletier entered parliament with Trudeau, insisting on entering as a threesome. Macdonald was largely responsible for persuading Trudeau that his candidacy as Liberal leader would be strongly supported in Ontario.

they regarded as the stultifying conduct of foreign policy under Martin.

It is rarely appreciated that Pearson as prime minister exerted little regular influence on the foreign policy of his government. True, he gave some memorable speeches such as that at Temple University (Philadelphia) in 1965 advocating a suspension of the bombing attacks in North Vietnam. (It was symptomatic of his unusual relationship with Martin that the latter was not shown the text of this dramatic speech before its delivery.) Pearson's intervention was also decisive in some situations such as the offer of peacekeeping forces for Cyprus. But the continuing direction of foreign policy came very much from the responsible minister.

Martin was well prepared for his post. On first being elected to parliament in 1935 he had visited Geneva as an observer at the League of Nations; he had headed Canadian delegations to the UN in the St Laurent government. Not only did he know his subject; he was a superb tactician in getting his own way. Finally, he had been runner-up in the leadership race of 1957 and Pearson accorded him a special position in his cabinet, which the minister skilfully exploited. Pearson was, moreover, preoccupied with a series of domestic crises which left him no time for the consistent pursuit of international affairs.

These were the factors which Paul Martin utilized in preserving the foreign policy he believed in. His principal technique, already described, was to avoid bringing up issues in the cabinet where he might be pressed for change and instead to take them directly to the prime minister, which left him free to beat a retreat if Pearson's reaction was unfavourable. Being extraordinarily well read, with a strong belief in internationalism and a sense of responsibility, Martin used his great tactical skill to reduce to a minimum those concessions to popular instinct which must be made in any democracy. Pearson would from time to time suggest changes, influenced in part by developing pressures around him. Hence the proposal for a bombing halt in Vietnam. Hence also his advocacy from time to time of a reduction in Canada's contribution to NATO. As early as 1965, in a lecture to the Institute for Strategic Studies he had spoken of the need for more European direction within

NATO, arguing that ' this would make possible some with-drawal of United States and Canadian involvement in the European side of NATO '. But in each instance Martin, often by coming up with some new proposal for procedural review, would be able to resist the pressure for what he regarded as popular concessions.

As long as Martin remained secretary of state for external affairs, this approach worked. But the cost was increasing alienation and frustration on the part of Trudeau and some of his colleagues, who felt that Martin was deliberately preventing them from exercising the influence to which they were entitled as ministers. When they took over, they were determined on change. Trudeau refused Martin's request to remain as foreign minister, offering him instead the leadership of the Senate. This removed him from his power base. As the minister of the environment, Jack Davis, remarked to the Senate Committee on Foreign Affairs, in answering criticism of the government's decision to proceed unilaterally to establish fisheries closing lines: ' Senator Martin and others have argued very strongly the same position as you have argued and while they were in positions of power their views obtained ';[2] quite a pointed remark for a minister to make to other Senators about a col-league still a member of the cabinet and government leader in the Senate!

Anxious to avoid similar frustrations in his own cabinet, Trudeau has sought the development of a genuine system of cabinet scrutiny of all government policy. In a television inter-view he described in characteristically academic terms his ideas on how government should work:

... I think it important to create confidence in the people about the ability of this society to work out its problems. Creating confidence really means talking, explaining. It's having a seminar all the time, with Parliament, with Cabinet, with the caucus, with the country. ... It's looking for better solutions and this, I suppose, is teaching.[3]

In the cabinet he has stimulated the questioning of underly-ing principles and encouraged ministers to challenge the views of the ministers directly responsible. This is a dramatic change.

[2] Parl., Senate, Standing Cttee on Foreign Affairs, *Proc.*, 9 Mar. 1971, p. 20.
[3] CBC-TV interview, 2 Jan. 1969.

Formerly departmental ministers would in effect agree not to challenge the recommendations of their colleagues (except where these might jeopardize the future of the party or the government) in exchange for a free hand in their own domains. By upsetting this unwritten practice Trudeau diminished the strength ministers have derived from heading major departments, increased the relative strength of the articulate, intelligent, well-informed, and well-prepared cabinet minister, and, most of all, enlarged his own freedom of manoeuvre.

In this context the prime minister's unusual but deliberate stimulation of public debate on the future of Canada's position in NATO is perfectly explicable. Contrary to strongly established traditions of cabinet government in Canada, the prime minister encouraged his ministers to speak their minds in public. Gradually they responded. The then minister of defence and the secretary of state for external affairs, perhaps over-confident that the majority in cabinet, parliament, and the country favoured the maintenance at existing levels of Canadian forces in Europe, increasingly committed themselves to such a policy. Eric Kierans, at that time postmaster-general who later resigned from the cabinet, came out strongly for total withdrawal from NATO. Within the cabinet there were other partisans of both schools.

The prime minister widened the circle of participants when he announced that the government would hold up its decision until the Commons Standing Committee on External Affairs and National Defence returned from Europe in March 1969, and reported to the House. That committee added to the prime minister's problems by advocating the maintenance of existing force levels. A cabinet meeting extending throughout a whole weekend in late March failed to compose differences. The following Thursday, 3 April 1969, the prime minister was finally able to cajole the cabinet into agreeing with the statement of policy which he and his personal advisers had drafted in the interval committing the government to ' a planned and phased reduction of the size of the Canadian forces in Europe '.[4]

This whole episode illustrated also the prime minister's determination and skill. On a major matter of policy, with the

4 Office of PM, press release, 3 Apr. 1969.

two ministers principally responsible, most of the senior civil service, the House Committee, an important segment of caucus and public opinion (according to a Gallup poll 64 per cent of Canadians opposed force reductions in Europe), all against him, he still went ahead and prevailed. Trudeau's success cannot, of course, be ascribed uniquely to this technique of encouraging free debate in cabinet. His personal triumph in the election of 1968, won without committing himself to any men or any specific policies, has left him with far fewer debts than is normal in political life. But his subsequent handling of government business has been deliberately designed to maximize that independence.

Another dramatic demonstration of this special position was the decision announced in October 1969 to open a mission to the Vatican. Because of the strong opposition of several Protestant groups in Canada, in particular the Orangemen, previous governments had declined to enter into direct relations, even though by time of the 1961 census 46 per cent of the population was Roman Catholic. Moreover, the Vatican has had a papal representative in Ottawa since 1899, and reciprocal representation had been actively sought through the years, especially by Catholic groups from Quebec. Of late, Protestant opposition had greatly moderated. Equally, however, the Catholic impetus had diminished, particularly since the election of the rather conservative Paul VI as Pope. Nevertheless, Trudeau seems to have decided in 1969 that, even if there were only a few French Canadians who still felt that the federal government had been neglectful his government should remove this grievance. One has to speculate because the public reason given for the decision —that ' the Vatican is essentially about the cheapest listening post in the world. . . . We think the Vatican will give us much more grass roots information about the countries of the world than . . . particular posts which we will have to close ',[5] cannot be taken seriously, especially from a man who has publicly questioned the value of diplomacy as a career. It was certainly a question no longer being strongly debated in any significant quarter, including by the Roman Catholics in Canada. Many ministers—though not holding strong views—considered the

[5] Office of PM, transcript of press conference, 15 Oct. 1969.

timing bad, the more so because the announcement immediately followed a government decision to close seven foreign missions, including Berlin, for reasons of economy.

A characteristic of Trudeau's which can cause surprise is his remarkable public candour in acknowledging difficult situations. While flying back from his visit to the USSR, he was interviewed by a group of accompanying journalists. Asked if he had pressed the Soviet leaders for the release of imprisoned Ukranian nationalists, as urged to do by Ukrainian Canadian organizations, he observed:

My position in the Soviet Union or in Canada is that anyone who breaks the law in order to assert his nationalism doesn't get much sympathy from me. But I didn't feel like bringing up any case which would have caused Mr Brezhnev or Mr Kosygin to say . . . ' Why should you put your revolutionaries in jail and we shouldn't put ours?' [6]

Predictably, the Ukrainian Canadian community reacted with anger and dismay. Within a week the prime minister found himself receiving a delegation of Ukrainian group leaders, whom he was able to some degree to placate by pointing out that he had been accompanied to Russia by a Ukrainian Canadian MP, Walter Deakon, who had appealed in Ukrainian to the leaders of the Ukrainian Republic in Kiev for the freedom of relatives to join their families in Canada. As for the offending statement, he said only that he had been ' misrepresented '.

The anger of the Ukrainian Canadians can be explained in part by their conviction that the Trudeau government is more concerned over the Canadian Jewish vote, which goes overwhelmingly to the Liberals, than with the Ukrainian vote which, although much larger, has been largely Conservative since Diefenbaker's premiership. Ukrainian Canadians felt that in the Soviet Union these considerations had led Trudeau to give more support to Jewish emigration and the release of Jewish prisoners—which the Jewish community in Canada had urged him to advocate—than to Ukrainian causes. In fact, one

[6] Office of PM, transcript of PM's interview with press and radio reporters en route to Ottawa from Soviet visit, 28 May 1971.

imagines that the interests of neither group figured prominently in the prime minister's private representations, but he did show more caution in reporting on his advocacy of the Jewish causes.

It is, moreover, an important factor in Canada's international posture that it has constantly shown more sympathy for Israeli than for Arab positions in the Middle East conflict. While Canada was a member of UNEF in the Middle East, a supreme and not always successful effort was made to maintain a neutral stance. But since the expulsion of UNEF in 1967, there has been no strong argument for restraint, and the well-organized Jewish lobby in Canada has pressed relentlessly for support of Israel and of Jews in Russia on every occasion. The remarkable influence of Canadian Jews comes less from their numbers— about 175,000 in 1961—than from their wealth, their financial support of the Liberal party, their superb organization, and their concentration in the large cities which vote Liberal.[7] Their relative impact is the greater because there are fewer Arabs in Canada, and they are, moreover, dispersed, divided among different religions and sects, less well organized, and much less wealthy.

As a result, Canada's potential to play a useful peacekeeping role in the Middle East, if the need should again arise, may have diminished. Canada is hardly likely to be acceptable to the Arab states. The situation is self-generating because, as J. L. Granatstein has said, ' the press is overwhelmingly sympathetic to Israel and sometimes openly biased in its favour '. This same commentator has written critically of the fact ' that North American Jews have got themselves into the position where they are bound to support Israel regardless of its policies ', and he has suggested that ' a healthy critical spirit . . . may even be in the best interests of Canadian Jewry '.[8] Given these domestic circumstances and the intractability of Arab-Israeli relations, the government has probably taken the wisest course in leaving the resolution of the Middle East conflict to the four permanent members of the Security Council and in limiting its public position to support of the Council's resolution 242 of November

[7] The constituencies of the prime minister and of the secretary of state for external affairs have by coincidence the two largest proportions of Jewish votes in Canada.

[8] J. L. Granatstein, *Canadian Forum*, June 1971, p. 35.

1967, which falls far short of satisfying Canadian Jewish pressure groups.

Trudeau has remained an avid traveller and he has made more and longer visits during his three years in office than any of his predecessors. He was in London for the Commonwealth Conference in January 1969, with a quick side visit to Rome and the Vatican; to Washington in March 1969; to the Far East, including Japan, Malaysia, Singapore, Hong Kong, Australia, and New Zealand in May 1970; to the Singapore Commonwealth Conference with visits to Pakistan, India, Indonesia, and Ceylon in January 1971; and to the Soviet Union in May 1971. These journeys naturally convey the impression abroad that the prime minister is deeply interested in foreign affairs. Curiosity he has, particularly for non-Western societies, but Trudeau's real interests and commitment are to national problems. He takes an interest in foreign affairs normally only when he is actually out of the country. While in Canada he devotes little time to them. He also strongly resists the normal protocol or symbolic manifestations of his position. He will rarely agree to receive visiting foreign ministers or other prominent delegations from abroad and he could not be persuaded to speak at the UN on the occasion of the twenty-fifth anniversary.

Presidents and prime ministers have taken an increasingly active part in the formulation of their nation's foreign policies. Trudeau quite obviously does not conform to this trend. While he holds some views strongly and has shown determination in achieving some foreign policy goals, he is normally content to leave the elaboration and execution of policy to his secretary of state for external affairs, Mitchell Sharp. Given the prime minister's authority and his unconventionality, Sharp's position has not always been easy. He began with the disadvantage that he had run as a candidate for Liberal leader, but conceded to Trudeau only a few days before the convention. The first two major issues with which he had to deal, NATO and Biafra, both caused him trouble and there were many who predicted that he would be replaced. But Mitchell Sharp is a man of great experience in government; he was formerly a deputy minister [9] in the

[9] Equivalent to UK permanent under-secretary.

Department of Trade and Commerce and subsequently a minister in that department and later of Finance. The prime minister has obviously found Sharp's experience of value, particularly in the complex field of foreign economic policy, an area of great importance to Canada in which previous foreign ministers have all lacked specific competence. Thus Sharp has confounded the prophets and has emerged as a business-like manager of Canadian foreign policy.

If foreigners have found it difficult to understand Trudeau's personal style, the Canadian foreign service has had just as much trouble. For a generation this had been the elite corps among Canadian civil servants and had been equally respected abroad. Sir William Hayter has written ' of the Canadians, who so brilliantly built up from nothing one of the highest-powered Foreign Services in the modern world '.[10] But within a year of Trudeau's election very different comments were being made. Professor James Eayrs was advocating nothing less than ' a radical reorganization of the Department of External Affairs. The name is External not Eternal. Most of its postings are expendable. Much of its work is redundant. Many of its officials unnecessary.'[11]

In the minds of Canadian foreign-service officers, the prime minister had encouraged these attacks with his own expression of doubt about the role of the diplomat in the latter half of the twentieth century. Referring to diplomacy as outmoded, he remarked: ' I believe it all goes back to the early days of the telegraph when you needed a dispatch to know what was happening in country A, whereas now most of the time you can read it in a good newspaper.'[12] Suspicion of the prime minister's intentions was stimulated by his evident disregard of official advice during the review of Canada's future role in NATO, an entirely new experience for this elite service. The impact of these events, combined with the closing of seven missions and a 7 per cent reduction in personnel,[13] some with thirty years' service, had very adverse effects on morale.

[10] *The Diplomacy of the Great Powers* (London, 1960), p. 65.
[11] *Toronto Star*, 10 Sept. 1969.
[12] CBC-TV interview, 1 Jan. 1969.
[13] A. E. Ritchie, Parl., H. of C. SCEAND, *Mins & Proc. of Evidence*, 7 Apr. 1970, p. 15.

Although the Department of External Affairs had faced a difficult period of adjustment during Diefenbaker's premiership, the foreign service felt that it had ridden out those years with its personnel, and therefore its potential, almost intact, and that in the process Canada's international standing had been maintained through cautious retrenchment in some areas of activity. Thus, although Diefenbaker never trusted the foreign service, they in turn felt he had never beaten them. There are, indeed, certain parallels to the demoralizing situation in which the British foreign service found itself following the Suez invasion, when, after the first instinct of so many to resign had been resisted, the entire service decided in an almost corporate manner that they had to maintain solidarity to restore Britain's international position.

Professional foreign-service officers knew when Diefenbaker was elected that they were in for a hard time. They were forewarned by his campaign promise to do the impossible and reverse the downward trend in Britain's share of Canada's foreign trade. With Trudeau there were no such warnings of trouble ahead. He was welcomed by most members of the service for his refreshing, pragmatic, outgoing approach to the world. They were not prepared for the attitude of suspicion of the foreign service held by many of the new ministers who came in with Trudeau. Too long an elite, the service had become insensitive to the reactions of politicians and other government departments in Ottawa. Their reaction, when they found themselves in trouble, was to employ the tactic which had worked with Diefenbaker. But they discovered that in Trudeau they were dealing with a tougher, more determined, and better organized man, one intent on achieving change where he considered it necessary.

Apart from his conviction that Canadian foreign policy needed bringing up to date, the prime minister believed that an unreasonably large number of able persons with talents badly needed in the domestic sector of government was cooped up in the Department of External Affairs. One effect, deliberate or accidental, of his downgrading of the foreign service has been that in his first three years of office, a surprising number of foreign service officers have accepted senior positions in other government departments. More specifically, one in every three deputy ministers, as well as a number of assistant deputy ministers and highly placed advisers in the Offices of the Privy Council and the prime minister are former members of the Canadian foreign service. Of these, more than half have left External Affairs since 1968.

This unparalleled outflow has probably had a salutary effect within the foreign service, providing opportunities for younger officers to acquire more challenging responsibilities than would otherwise have been possible. Time has worked its cure in other ways, too. The prime minister had no desire to destroy the foreign service—as many of its members suspected—but only to cut it down to size, and this has now been done. The completion of the foreign-policy review has also helped to bring the government and the department into greater harmony. The central, effective, and much appreciated role of the Departments of External Affairs and National Defence—which had also felt under fire after the NATO cuts—in the crisis occasioned by the kidnapping of the diplomat James Cross in October 1970 has also done much to restore internal morale.

The surest sign of a newly gained self-confidence is the way in which the Department has responded to the potentially far-reaching plans to move towards the integration of government operations abroad, and possibly eventually of the responsible ministries in Ottawa. This was announced in the foreign-policy review of 1971 (*Foreign Policy for Canadians*):

To meet the challenges of coming decades, to be equipped to take advantage of new opportunities, to keep abreast of the rapid evolution of events, the Government needs a strong and flexible organization for carrying out its reshaped foreign policy. . . . The Government has decided that there should be maximum integration in its foreign operations that will effectively contribute to the achievement of national objectives (p. 39).

Instead of seeing this as a threat to be resisted, the Department has taken it as a challenge to be explored, carefully but imaginatively. It is too early to know where this programme will lead. The only modest step taken so far has been integration of support services abroad. But the Department of External

Affairs is clearly once again an effective instrument for the execution under ministerial direction of Canadian foreign policy.

3

CANADA'S PERCEPTION OF THE EXTERNAL THREAT

In the two decades which followed World War II Canadians almost without exception shared the perception of Western Europeans that they faced a common threat from the Soviet Union. Canadians had been enthusiastic converts to the principle of collective security as embodied in the North Atlantic Treaty. This conversion was a direct consequence of unavoidable involvement in two European wars, which Canada in no way caused. Thus Canadians were already prepared when the cold war developed in the late 1940s to regard Europe as Canada's first line of defence and to contribute important quantities of men and equipment in the early 1950s to its defence. Subsequently, as the Soviet Union developed nuclear weapons and acquired a modest intercontinental bomber force, Canadians realized, as Lester Pearson put it, that the country was ' in the dangerous position of being sandwiched geographically between the USSR and the United States '.[1] It was then natural to enter into the NORAD (North American Air Defence) agreement with the United States to provide an integrated defence against possible Soviet bomber attacks.

These arrangements within NATO and within NORAD no longer command the general support they once did. The Soviet threat is not now the overwhelming concern that it once was. Indeed, many Canadians have recently been preoccupied with the United States and France than with the Soviet Union as a source of external danger. Twenty years of armed peace have lessened the fear of a Soviet drive into Western Europe. More generally, many Canadians now regard Europeans as able, with US nuclear support, to provide an adequate defence of their continent. This attitude has been stimulated by the well-advertised achievements of the EEC, the industrial and financial successes of Germany, France, and

[1] *Globe and Mail* (Toronto), 22 Feb. 1947.

(until recently) Italy, resentment over the EEC's Common Agricultural Policy, and by the clear evidence that Britain is putting national interest foremost in negotiating its way into the Common Market. Indeed, it is a prevalent Canadian view that West Europeans are selfish and become interested in Canada only at moments when there is a prospect that Canadian forces in Europe may be reduced. This has moved a man as moderate and generous as John Holmes to complain:

It is ironical that those Western European (including British) Ministers who do so much huffing and puffing about something called ' Europe ', about ' its ' rights and ' its ' interests and ' its ' voice, feel no shame in reprimanding a non-European country of middle size for not being willing to go on defending Europe indefinitely.[2]

At this stage the most persuasive and generally accepted argument for a continuing Canadian military contribution to Europe is the assertion that Canada needs some link with Europe to balance the United States, and that from the European standpoint the most welcome form of Canadian connection is a defence contribution.

Defence links with the United States, symbolized by the NORAD agreement, have likewise come in for increasing public questioning in Canada. Canadian frustration and resentment over US involvement in Vietnam are probably the primary cause. Canada, the closest neighbour and friend of the United States, has through its government been more critical of US military action in Vietnam than has any West European government, except those of France and Sweden. This has not been an easy position for Canadian governments, aware of the overriding importance of maintaining the friendship of the United States and of continuing to co-operate in the integrated continental defence arrangements to which the Americans naturally attach importance. Moreover, Canadians, because of their physical and cultural proximity to Americans, tend to become involved in their internal debates: yet not being Americans and not participating in the Vietnam war, their judgement is not warped by considerations of pride and patriotism. Thus, while numbers of Canadians strongly support US

[2] ' Canadian Foreign Policy ', *The World Today*, Oct. 1969, p. 456.

involvement in Vietnam—to the extent of demonstrating in support of the war when similar demonstrations are being held in American cities and of volunteering, at one time [3] in sizeable numbers, to fight with US forces in Vietnam—the great majority of Canadians oppose the war. Many feel embarrassed over Canadian sales of military supplies to the United States under the Defence Production Sharing Agreement negotiated in 1959. Because undetermined amounts of these supplies are sent to Vietnam, there are strong voices and important national organizations pressing for the banning of all such sales.

The evolving nature of the military confrontation of the superpowers has also had its effect on support in Canada for co-operation with the United States in continental defence. When the need for an active defence of the continent against a possible bomber attack arose in the early 1950s Canadians would have preferred to have continental defence arrangements subsumed under NATO command, for, with Britain, France, and the United States all members of NATO, Canada has been able to deal jointly with the three countries with whom close ties are necessary and yet sensitive. But the United States declined to permit its European allies to participate in continental defence, and so at sea and in the air bilateral arrangements with Canada were developed. As the speed of intercontinental bombers increased, so these defence arrangements became more and more interwoven, until the NORAD agreement of 1958 established a fully-integrated continental air-defence scheme.

Because of the special sensitivity of Canadians to the United States, this has never been a popular agreement. But as long as it provided a credible defence against a nuclear attack on the continent, it could not be seriously challenged. With the development of a major Soviet ICBM capability, bomber defence has become more and more secondary. It is, however, self-evident that the United States will insist on maintaining some kind of continental bomber defence. For this purpose the use of Canadian air space and ground facilities is important, although not absolutely essential, because it permits a forward defence against an attack which would inevitably come from the north.

[3] US army regulations now effectively prevent this practice.

Canadian governments have accordingly concluded that co-operation with the United States in air defence preserves Canadian sovereignty from a possible US challenge and avoids a confrontation which could threaten the multitudinous other forms of mutually beneficial co-operation between the two countries. But at a time when the whole continent lies unprotected from a Soviet missile attack, the necessity of maintaining an elaborate defence against 150 ageing Soviet bombers is not easy to justify.

A similar argument applies in the field of maritime defence. Here Canada has concentrated on anti-submarine warfare (ASW) and has developed a highly competent and advanced ASW force which co-operates closely with the Americans off both the Atlantic and Pacific coasts. This force was designed primarily to protect the Atlantic shipping lanes from diesel-powered submarines, and in this role it provided a relatively effective defence. But in the last few years the nature of the Soviet submarine challenge has changed completely. Now the threat is from nuclear-powered submarines equipped with nuclear-armed missiles similar to the American Polaris. Against these weapons, Canada's ASW forces can at best make it difficult for Soviet submarines to lie undetected close to the North American coastline. But this does not provide a strong political justification for the emphasis which has prevailed to date on the ASW role, with its close tie-in with the Americans, particularly when there is no defence against Soviet land-based missiles. That there has been less criticism of this co-operative defence activity than of air defence probably relates less to differing judgements of the efficacy of the two roles—for there is in fact little to choose between them—and more to the less obtrusive character of maritime forces. Large naval expenditures in the maritime provinces, one of the more economically depressed regions of Canada, undoubtedly also account for the strong regional support which the maritime forces have received.

The Cuban crisis of 1962 likewise has had its effect on Canadian attitudes towards defence co-operation with the United States. Unlike the countries of Western Europe, which could share General de Gaulle's appreciation that this was an American problem to be handled as the US president judged best, Canada was inextricably involved as soon as the US government decided to put NORAD on standby alert. NORAD's integrated character meant that this order implicated Canadian forces. Yet Canada was consulted no earlier and no more fully than the European allies. More recently, whenever US action in the Far East has seemed to involve a risk of wider escalation, this concern over automatic involvement has manifested itself and added to the argument of those advocating an end to these integrated defence links.[4]

In recent years, a strong faction within the United States has come to favour the development of a ballistic-missile defence system for the United States. As now conceived, this system would be based exclusively on US territory, so that—unlike the bomber defence system—no direct Canadian involvement is needed. Given the sensitivity of Canadian opinion in this area, this is fortunate. Indeed, while no proponents in Canada of involvement in the US programme have emerged, there is a concerned minority which is actively opposed to it. Such controversy as has developed in Canada therefore is over the question whether the Canadian government should stand quietly apart or publicly criticize and dissociate itself from US plans.

East-West relations

In the wider debate Canadians tend to think in terms of possible political and disarmament measures as a constructive approach to East–West confrontation in Europe. Within NATO, Canadians have traditionally favoured measures aimed at promoting détente to the point that Paul-Henri Spaak observed privately during a visit to Ottawa in 1958 that ' Canadians are the Yugoslavs of NATO '. It was no accident that the first visit by a NATO foreign minister to the Soviet Union was undertaken by Pearson in 1955.

During the following years, particularly while Diefenbaker was prime minister, this policy of trying to break down barriers with the countries of the Soviet bloc was frustrated by internal politics. In foreign policy, the then secretary of state for external

---

[4] For instance, the president of the Canadian Labour Congress testified before the H. of C. SCEAND on 23 Feb. 1971 that his organization called upon the government ' to withhold the provision of material of war supplied [under this agreement] for utilization in the Vietnam conflict '.

affairs, Howard Green, was committed, somewhat naïvely perhaps, to the search for disarmament. But any political benefit in
terms of rapprochement with the countries of Eastern Europe
which this policy might have achieved was more than over-
balanced by Diefenbaker's efforts to court Canadians of East
European origin. Canada has sizeable concentrations of East
European immigrants who came in three main waves: before
World War I, during the interwar period, and after World War
II. Even after two generations in Canada they have retained to
a remarkable extent their cultural identity, and as many as
possible of their links with their families in the countries from
which they came.

Their numbers, including descendants, are quite large: in
1961 there were 473,000 Canadians of Ukrainian origin,
324,000 of Polish origin, 73,000 of Czechoslovak origin, 28,000
of Lithuanian origin, 126,000 of Hungarian origin, 44,000 of
Rumanian origin, 69,000 of Serbo-Croat origin, and 119,000 of
Russian origin.[5] The total amounted to 7·0 per cent of the
Canadian population. Since these groups tended to be concentrated geographically, they formed a significant electoral
force in perhaps one-third of all constituencies.

Diefenbaker, an instinctive politician from the West, where
East European immigrants are concentrated, associated himself
closely with the nationalist and militant anti-communist views
of these groups, the organized leadership of which has tended to
fall into the hands of strong anti-communists. In the main, his
efforts took the form of making vigorous anti-communist and
anti-Soviet statements at their many ceremonies and meetings
in Canada. This practice was carefully watched by the embassies
of the USSR and the other East European countries and
regularly elicited complaints which seemed to be without
effect.

In November 1961, however, Diefenbaker went much further, publicly announcing his intention to instruct the Canadian
delegation to the General Assembly to introduce a resolution
condemning Soviet ' colonialism '. In the end he was persuaded
not to do so, but only after very high-level interventions from
the British and American governments.

[5] *Canada Year Book 1968* (Dominion Bureau of Statistics), p. 208.

After 1963 the new Liberal government under Lester Pearson resumed the traditional emphasis on bridge-building with the Soviet world. Paul Martin, then secretary of state for external affairs, visited the USSR in November 1966, during which he sought to engage the Soviet leaders in discussion of the principal international issues of the day such as Vietnam. But by this time Khrushchev had visited the United States and Western leaders were frequent visitors to the Soviet Union, so that Canada's approach had become rather routine. Trudeau gave new impetus to Soviet-Canadian relations by making an extended visit to the USSR in May 1971.[6] In his conversations with Kosygin and Brezhnev, there was naturally discussion of the larger international issues, such as balanced force reductions in Europe. But Trudeau showed little interest in playing the role of intermediary between the USSR and the West, as he indicated in a characteristically frank manner in Moscow on 20 May 1971: ' . . . I have never been particularly fond of the role of carrying messages from one party to another. I think people are able to do that for themselves.'[7]

He was much more concerned with bilateral relations and with how the development of those relations might affect Canada's view of its relations with the United States. In some rather informal comments, which have come in for a good deal of criticism in Canada, he said of his visit that it was:

pour nous . . . un pas important vers l'établissement d'une politique étrangère la plus autonome possible. Chacun sait que les Canadiens se sentent passablement dominés par la présence américaine et c'est important pour nous d'avoir d'autres interlocuteurs. . . . Je pense que c'est important pour nous, comme nation canadienne, d'avoir des ouvertures sur un pays qui, comme l'union soviétique, est certainement l'une des deux superpuissances. . . .[8]

These remarks must, of course, be seen in context, and account must be taken of the natural tendency to exaggerate the importance of one's host country, but they probably reflect the basic outlook and aspiration of the prime minister.

[6] Postponed from the previous October due to the kidnapping crisis in Quebec.
[7] Office of PM, transcript of prime minister's press conference, Moscow, 20 May 1971.
[8] Radio-Canada interview, Moscow, 20 May 1971.

While in Moscow Trudeau also signed a bilateral protocol calling for ' consultations on important international problems of mutual interest and on questions of bilateral relations '.[9] In applying this protocol the USSR may be expected to place the emphasis on international issues, but Canada will pursue the bilateral opportunities. The Canadian government sees this protocol, concluded a few months after the signature of an agreement ' on co-operation in the industrial application of science and technology ' (known as the Industrial Exchanges Agreement),[10] as part of a systematic programme for expanding Soviet-Canadian contacts and for diversifying Canada's international relationships. Other arrangements to facilitate exchanges with the USSR can be expected to follow.

Trudeau's own visit was deliberately designed to forward specific Canadian bilateral interests. He went to Norilsk and to Murmansk, both large northern cities. Norilsk in particular is of interest to Canadians and the prime minister showed by his personal attention some of the areas susceptible of continuing consultation under the protocol, such as housing and urban and industrial development in Arctic regions, the problems of ice-breaking, and the long-distance transmission of hydro-power. In all these activities Canada and the USSR face common technical problems, and co-operation outside of international politics should be possible. Indeed, less than three months since Trudeau's return, Jean Chrétien, the minister responsible for Indian Affairs and Northern Development, ended a three-week visit to the Soviet Arctic with an announcement that a joint Canadian-Soviet working group on Arctic scientific research was to be established.

Yet another indication of current Soviet interest in developing relations with Canada has been the surprisingly prompt return visit by Kosygin in October 1971. During his nine-day stay the two governments signed a General Exchanges Agreement intended to expand Canadian-Soviet exchanges in scientific, technical, educational, cultural, and other fields. A follow-up to the Industrial Exchanges Agreement, it sets up a

[9] USSR-Canada Protocol on Consultations, 19 May 1971.

[10] Signed by Jean-Luc Pepin, minister of industry, trade and commerce, in Moscow on 27 January 1971, but originally intended for signature during Trudeau's planned visit in Oct. 1970.

Canada–USSR mixed commission which is to meet every two years to work out and review programmes of exchanges.

This emphasis on tackling problems unique to the two countries provides an effective practical basis for dealing with the Soviet Union. It may even be that in the course of these and other co-operative activities some of the still-existing tension in East–West relations may be reduced, although if this occurs it will be a by-product rather than the main aim of contact as seen from the Canadian side. This approach is less effective with the other countries of Eastern Europe, with whom Canada does not share the same geographical and environmental problems. Nevertheless, Canada is expanding traditional forms of contact with them: visits by the secretary of state for external affairs to Yugoslavia and Rumania in May and June 1970, by the Polish foreign minister to Ottawa in October 1970, and a return visit by the Rumanian foreign minister in June 1971 and also a visit by President Tito of Yugoslavia in November 1971.[11]

Disarmament

One subject of importance to Canada brought up in all these encounters is disarmament. Canada has had a special interest in this problem since the end of the war. Through the accident of having participated in the tripartite (Britain, Canada, US) nuclear development programme, Canada emerged from the war with an advanced nuclear technology. The government publicly renounced any intention of embarking on a nuclear-weapons programme, but Canada was nevertheless invited, on the grounds of special competence, to join the members of the Security Council (excluding China) on the first UN disarmament negotiating forum, the Atomic Energy Commission. Canada has been a member of every multilateral disarmament body established since 1952. In fact, while Howard Green was Conservative minister of external affairs (1959–62), disarmament was his preoccupation, to the point that Canada became an object of suspicion and ridicule within NATO. But the opportunities for success were limited, and one of the few

[11] A meeting between Prime Minister Trudeau and President Tito had been scheduled for August 1971 in Yugoslavia but Trudeau decided to cancel the visit and return to Ottawa in the wake of President Nixon's surcharge measures of 15 August.

residues of Green's activity is the joint US-Soviet chairmanship of the Conference of the Committee on Disarmament (CCD), a concept he proposed when that conference first convened in March 1962.

The Trudeau government began by attaching considerable importance to the principle of disarmament negotiations. On 23 April 1969, in a defence policy statement in the House of Commons, the prime minister stated:

Canada's record at the Eighteen Nation Disarmament Conference is an outstanding one. . . . It is the intention of this government that our foreign policy should provide for a growing investment of intellectual resources in this important area, and that one of the most important foreign relations tasks in which Canada is engaged is that which is directed to arms limitation and disarmament.[12]

In contrast with Howard Green, however, the government has been balanced in its pursuit of disarmament opportunities. The Canadian delegation to the CCD was very active, to the point of infuriating the Americans, in pressing for changes in the text of the seabed disarmament treaty of 1970. It sought inclusion of international procedures available to governments to verify compliance with the treaty, and of provisions ensuring the protection of the rights of coastal states. Once this treaty (with the changes sought by Canada incorporated in it) was signed, the Canadian delegation began to press for a more comprehensive test-ban treaty by suggesting a very low ceiling on the size of underground tests. In September 1971 Canada went the last mile and advocated a test-ban treaty to cover all underground testing.

This activity is intended to maintain international confidence in the CCD as a worthy negotiating body. But the government recognizes that the Strategic Arms Limitation Talks (SALT) are the most important disarmament forum of the day and it is probably significant that *Foreign Policy for Canadians*, which appeared a year after the prime minister's statement just cited, is muted in its expression of support for disarmament:

Canadian policy should, therefore, seek to contribute . . . to the maintenance of a stable balance of mutual deterrence . . . and . . . to the reduction through negotiated arms-control measures of the

[12] H. of C. Deb., 3 Apr. 1969, p. 7870.

risks of nuclear conflict. In pursuing these objectives, competing but parallel exigencies of Canadian political, commercial and defence interests which are associated with the fundamentals of peace and security must be carefully calculated in the process of decision.[13]

It goes on to say that ' it was difficult to conceive of significant achievements in this field during the 1970s ' unless substantial progress were to be made in the SALT talks or other breakthroughs in arms control and disarmament realized. The marked difference in tone from Trudeau's earlier statement indicates that he now recognizes more clearly than when his government was first elected that Canadian opportunities for advancing disarmament are limited.

The extent and persistence of public pressure on the government to pursue an active disarmament policy was graphically demonstrated by the remarkable public response to the US decision to explode a five megaton nuclear device at an underground testing site on Amchitka in November 1971. This isolated Alaskan island is 1,500 miles from the closest point on the west coast of Canada. Yet in the weeks preceding the test there was a groundswell of protest by the Canadian public from coast to coast. Fears were expressed that such a test in a geographically unstable area could trigger an earthquake or cause a tidal wave or result in radioactive venting in the atmosphere above Canada or in delayed radioactive leakage into the ocean, perhaps decades later. The surprisingly massive public outcry expressed itself in various forms: demonstrations in front of American consulates across the country, including one group of 8,000 protesters in Toronto; petitions and telegrams addressed to Washington, one signed by over 170,000 Canadians; student demonstrators who temporarily and symbolically blocked the international crossing bridges at three Ontario border points, Sarnia, Windsor and Niagara Falls; two unsuccessful attempts by a west coast protest group to dramatize the situation by sailing their ship into the test area before the detonation took place; four major Canadian church groups appealing to President Nixon to halt the test; a telegram from the Ontario Federation of Labour on behalf of its 700,000 workers to the president urging that the test be called off; and a strongly

[13] *FPC: United Nations*, p. 14.

worded telegram from the Ontario minister of the environment to Nixon on behalf of ' eight million residents of Ontario who protest your decision ', which asked bluntly ' What more scientific knowledge can you gain by this affront to humanity ? ' [14]

From the outset, the federal government made its opposition to the American decision abundantly clear and stressed that ' Canada and other nations threatened will necessarily hold the United States responsible for any short or long term effects of the test '.[15] In the Commons in October only one member opposed[16] a resolution introduced by the secretary of state for external affairs, Mitchell Sharp:

Whereas the continued testing of nuclear warheads by the nuclear powers adds to the dangers of the nuclear arms race and may seriously pollute the human environment, and

Whereas the scheduled nuclear test of Amchitka is of particular concern to Canadians because of its proximity to Canada's west coast,

This Canadian House of Commons calls on all nuclear powers to cease all testing of nuclear devices, and particularly, calls on the President of the United States to cancel the test at Amchitka scheduled for this month.[17]

The opposition parties pressed strongly for Trudeau to intercede directly with the president, but he refused to do so, probably at some cost to his national popularity. However, the parliamentary secretary to the secretary of state for external affairs addressed the UN First Committee stressing Canada's particular concern for the Amchitka test ' because it is on our doorstep ', and its general concern to bring an end to the ' poisonous, dangerous, and in the ultimate, futile ' contest in which the superpowers were engaged.[18]

This vigorous outburst by the Canadian public to the Amchitka episode reflects a variety of concerns: broad interest in environmental questions, a growing scepticism that the United States really needed to improve on its already devastating nuclear capacity, a carry-over of opposition to US involvement

[14] *Globe and Mail*, 29 Oct. 1971.

[15] H. of C. Deb., 27 Oct. 1971, p. 9073.

[16] One Conservative member voted against the resolution on the grounds that the United States needed to maintain its deterrent power.

[17] H. of C. Deb., 15 Oct. 1971, p. 8735.

[18] Canadian Delegation to the UN, press release, 28 Oct. 1971.

in Vietnam, the persisting Canadian advocacy of détente
and disarmament, and more subtly perhaps, a national reaction
to apparent American indifference to the effect of Nixon's
tariff barriers on Canada. But whatever the causes, the force of
public opinion was too strong to be ignored.

Canada and NATO

In view of the government's early interest in disarmament,
it may seem surprising that no apparent account was taken at
the time of the possibilities for exploiting the withdrawal of
Canadian forces from Europe to promote an agreement on
balanced force reductions with the Russians. The argument,
in fact, has little strength because the USSR could not be
expected, initially at least, to equate Soviet and Canadian
troops. In any event, the Trudeau government reached its
decision to reduce Canadian forces in Germany because it no
longer regarded Europe, as its postwar predecessors all did,
as Canada's first line of defence. It was ready to maintain a
small Canadian contribution to NATO in Europe as proof of a
continuing Canadian commitment to the principle of collective
defence and in the belief that ' Europe is still probably the most
sensitive point in the East–West balance of power '. But the
emphasis in the government's new White Paper, *Defence in the
70s*, is on the assertion that ' NATO's collective defence rests
primarily on defence of national homelands '. In defending the
decision to reduce Canadian forces in Europe, which are to be
maintained at their present level of 5,000 men, comprising a
highly mobile battalion group and three squadrons of CF-104s
to be employed in the conventional attack role, the White Paper
notes that ' Canada is one of only two partners in the NATO
alliance which station forces outside their own continent . . .
[and] one of only six . . . which station forces outside their
national borders for NATO purposes '. The White Paper also
draws attention to the fact that at the time Canada reduced its
forces in Europe from 10,000 to 5,000 men, ' forces based in
Canada for emergency deployment to Europe were not reduced '
(pp. 32–5). These forces are not insignificant, comprising a
battalion group for deployment by Canadian military transport
aircraft within a week to Norway or Denmark for service with

the Allied Command Europe's Mobile Force (AMF), with the balance of the brigade to be available within a month. Indeed these home-based forces are now to be augmented by the commitment of two squadrons of CF-5 aircraft to support the two ground units already committed. Although based in Canada, these CF-5 aircraft can be rapidly flown across the Atlantic using Canadian jet transports for in-flight refuelling. One other decision, with implications for future Canadian defence cooperation with Europe, has been the agreement to make a training ground in western Canada available on a long-term basis to Britain and to begin negotiations with West Germany for a similar arrangement.

This reconfiguration of Canada's contribution to NATO, with its emphasis on home-based forces, is likely to set the pattern for the future. The Trudeau government has consciously accorded priority to home defence and to the defence of North America:

We shall maintain appropriate defence forces which will be designed to undertake the following roles: (a) the surveillance of our own territory and coast lines, i.e. the protection of our sovereignty; (b) the defence of North America in cooperation with United States forces; (c) the fulfillment of such NATO commitments as may be agreed upon; and (d) the performance of such international peacekeeping roles as we may from time to time assume.[19]

In spite of some public criticism the Trudeau government has remained committed to the principle of integrated continental defence. But recent events are emphasizing new requirements. The crisis which began with the kidnapping of James Cross in the autumn of 1970 has shown the need for some forces to provide internal security. At the same time opposition abroad to some of Canada's recent decisions to extend Canadian maritime authority for the purposes of fisheries conservation and control of pollution emphasizes the need for forces capable of surveying these extended areas of national responsibility and for exercising Canadian power in them. These latter requirements have been reviewed in *Defence in the 70s*. The principal innovation will be the establishment of

operations centres on the East and West coasts which will work

[19] Office of PM, press release, 3 Apr. 1969.

closely with the [responsible] civil departments to co-ordinate sur-veillance and control activities. . . . The Canadian Forces will carry out surveillance and exercise control in those areas not covered by the civil departments (p. 11).

In addition the White Paper expands on a theme which has been played down since World War II, the potential of the armed forces ' to contribute to the social and economic development of Canada ' (p. 12).

While this emphasis on the protection of Canadian sover-eignty might seem to diminish the relative importance accorded to the North American integrated defence, in practice it has led to only one small change in the equipment[20] of Canadian forces or in the functions they have been fulfilling. This has been possible through double tasking: air and sea forces required for surveillance and control of Canadian territory can at the same time provide Canada's contribution to co-operative continental defence.

A significant decision taken at the time the White Paper was approved in the cabinet concerns future defence expenditure. The decision to reduce Canadian forces in Europe in 1969 had been accompanied by, and was in fact prompted by, a defence budget freeze. Léo Cadieux, the defence minister, announced in the House on 2 June 1969 that it was expected that defence spending, ' barring unexpected international developments . . . will be maintained for the next three years at its current dollar level '.[21] Inevitably, with current rates of inflation, this decision has forced further retrenchment in Canadian defence pro-grammes. By agreeing to a modest increase in expenditure before the three-year period had ended, the Trudeau govern-ment has implied that it is ready to maintain continued Canadian military activity at its present level.

---

[20] Canada will dismantle in 1972 the two nuclear-armed BOMARC anti-aircraft missile bases, the provision of which contributed directly to the fall of the Diefenbaker government. However, this will cause little difficulty with the United States since the system is now outmoded and the Americans are dismantling their own BOMARC bases.

[21] H. of C. Deb., 2 June 1969, p. 9306.

4

NEW STRAINS IN THE FEDERAL STRUCTURE

THE empty streets of Quebec City in October 1964 when Queen Elizabeth visited that city in the course of a Canadian tour first alerted the international community to a revival of the periodic tension between French and English Canadians. The kidnapping of James Cross and the murder of Quebec's labour minister, Pierre Laporte, in 1970 confirmed that this crisis is acute and drawn out. In fact, the Canadian federation is undergoing the supreme test of its 100-year history and it cannot be taken for granted that it will survive intact.

Strain within the federal structure of Canada begins, but does not end with Quebec. The enormous size and conflicting regional interests of various parts of Canada produce a constant tension which governments must take account of, a tension which is of the essence in a federal state. An assistant to a former minister of the Alberta provincial government complained that ' the federal government's perversion of the federative principle has done much to perpetuate the alienation of the West. The West wants the right to develop freely, creatively and in its own style '[1]. However, the relative size of the French Canadian community—which is concentrated in the province of Quebec—its sense of cultural identity, and its place in Canada's history have always given an extra dimension to dealing with Quebec.

The Quebec problem

The Quebec problem in Canada has been acute for about a decade. Until the defeat of the province's Union Nationale government in 1960, the efforts of reformist elements in Quebec were concentrated on attacking Premier Maurice Duplessis, who had combined a conservative economic policy, nationalist slogans, gerrymandering and patronage to hold power without

[1] J. Barr & O. Anderson, *The Unfinished Revolt* (Toronto, 1971), p. 59.

interruption in the postwar years. The complaint of the reform-
ers—who included Pierre Trudeau, then editor of a small but
influential periodical *Cité Libre*—was that, by resisting all
twentieth-century reforms in labour relations, education, and
social policy, the premier was perpetuating the dependent
position of French Canadians in Canada. Duplessis was finally
defeated, not by the ballot but by death, and in 1960 a Liberal
government was elected under Jean Lesage, a former federal
minister. He and his associates, including René Levesque, now
head of the separatist Parti Québécois, began what became
known as the Quiet Revolution. With the process of reform
under way, the critics in Quebec felt that the necessary obstacles
to change at home had been removed. They now set their sights
on improving the standing and significance of Quebec and of
French Canadians in Canada. In this endeavour France began
as a pawn. But the pawn was queened and for several years
acted as a destructive force on the Canadian political chess-
board.

The French Canadians derive almost entirely from the
60,000 settlers cut off in North America after the final conquest
of 1763. The growth in their numbers to approximately six
million in Canada (omitting the roughly two million who have
emigrated over the years to the United States) is a triumph of
procreation; the maintenance of their culture and identity a
triumph of survival. But the coincidence in the late 1950s of a
sudden fall in the birth-rate combined with the recent appearance of television as a new instrument of cultural penetration
has increased the alarm of Quebeckers over the danger of being
swamped by the English-speaking culture of the continent.

Immigration has become a big issue. Interestingly, few
French have emigrated to Canada over the years; the same is
true of French-speaking Swiss and Belgians. The largest number
of immigrants to Quebec province since World War II has been
Italians, and almost all—about 120,000—have settled in
Montreal. It has been discovered that the vast majority of these
Italian immigrants are assimilating to the English-speaking
minority of Montreal, as are most other immigrants. Projections
of present trends suggest that by 1980 Montreal could have an
English-speaking majority. Although the province of Quebec

will unquestionably remain predominantly French-speaking, the discovery that its largest city, its business, commercial, and intellectual heart, indeed the second largest French-speaking city of the world, was in danger of losing its French-language majority, caused a severe psychological shock. As a consequence the government of Quebec is trying to require all students in the province to acquire a working knowledge of French as well as to influence immigration from abroad into the province and even the free movement into the professions from other parts of Canada.

Quebeckers have also become increasingly sensitive to the predominance of English-speaking Canadians in businesses located in Quebec. Though many businesses with nation-wide or continent-wide operations have their head offices in Montreal, this profession did not in the past attract French Canadians, whose classical training inclined them rather to law, medicine, and the priesthood. This situation is now evolving rapidly as a result of the university economics courses in the French language which have been offered since 1942. Within the last few years the Quebec government has also been searching desperately for ways of requiring companies located in Quebec to conduct their local operations in French without driving out capital or dis-couraging new capital from coming in—because Quebec needs external investments to generate increased employment.

Similar motives have led Quebec to try to gain control of broadcasting. There is already a French network within the national radio and television system which principally serves Quebec. While this service enjoys considerably autonomy—and is often alleged to harbour separatists, or at best strong French Canadian nationalists—it reports to the federal parliament. At one stage in the last decade the Quebec government announced that it was participating in a French television satellite enter-prise in order to achieve a direct link-up with French national television and that local projection would be organized pro-vincially. Cost has forced a delay in this proposal, but Maurice Schumann, the French foreign minister, stated in October 1971 that there had been no modification in the joint planning for this subject. Communications is indeed likely to be an area of continuing tension between Ottawa and Quebec City. Only very recently the provincial government announced a decision to establish an educational television system and to exercise provincial control over cable distribution. Jean-Paul L'Allier, the Quebec minister of communications, has taken a strongly nationalist stand, albeit within the Canadian federation, demanding ' legislative priority ' for Quebec in the field. He is quoted as saying that it was a question of national (meaning Quebec's) survival that the provincial government should have ultimate responsibility for policy in all the communications media. ' New communications, just as social policy, just as a cultural and education policy, are an essential element in the protection and development of Quebec, so that it can continue to be a positive contribution to Canada ', he said.[2] In support of his policy, he pointed out that in the EEC countries, the central government which he suggested was in the process of being formed would never touch cultural questions in the member countries.

These conditions within the province of Quebec prompted the Lesage government to turn to France for help in strengthening the French cultural fact in Canada. Initially this approach was welcomed and even encouraged by Ottawa. In the 200 years since the British conquest France had virtually ignored its former colony, and educated Frenchmen adopted a provoking and painfully evident superiority toward the culture of French Canada. For a long time this disdain was reciprocated by the majority of French Canadians, who remained loyal to the pre-revolutionary traditions of a church-based society. Change began perhaps with World War II, when some French took refuge in Quebec and came to appreciate the achievement of the French Canadian in preserving a French culture in North America. Thus in the 1960s both sides—France and Quebec—were ready to respond to the other.

What began as a marriage of convenience soon became a tempestuous affair. General de Gaulle in particular seemed determined to compensate for the years of scorn and neglect. In Quebec this interest was exploited by nationalists seeking ever greater autonomy. France in turn abetted these aspirations, stimulated perhaps by an instinctive anti-Anglo-Americanism

[2] *Globe and Mail*, 29 Nov. 1971.

which saw in English-speaking Canada a mélange of its two chief rivals of the day. Exploiting the ambiguity of words like *nation* in French (which in addition to the English meaning of country also means culturally distinct people), both France and Quebec developed a rhetoric and a diplomatic practice which pretended to a distinct and internationally recognized Quebec international personality.

Under President de Gaulle and Premier Lesage's successor, Daniel Johnson,[3] this game was taken to extreme lengths. In Ottawa encouragement turned first to toleration, then to increasing suspicion; communication between the governments of Ottawa and Quebec became practically non-existent and Ottawa started to take defensive action internationally. Quebec, in February 1965, had faced Ottawa with a cultural entente it had decided to sign with France, which the Canadian government, by an exchange of letters with the French ambassador, accepted. In November 1965, however, Ottawa concluded an *accord-cadre* with France under which future ententes would fall. It was intended as a kind of umbrella for direct contacts between Quebec and France, but these cultural contacts soon began to multiply without the federal government having the means of controlling their extent or even their character.

To forestall any possibility of the development of similar difficulties with Belgium, Ottawa decided to negotiate a bilateral cultural agreement in order to establish a framework for contact. Quebec was only officially consulted a few days before the agreement was to be signed in May 1967 in the presence of Prince Albert, a factor which may have been interpreted in Quebec as a provocative demonstration of Ottawa's international power. In retaliation the Quebec premier announced that he would boycott a dinner for the Belgian prince at Expo in Montreal. He was only persuaded to change his mind on the day of the dinner by the personal intervention of the prime minister, Pearson.

Ottawa also moved vigorously to extend its foreign-aid programme to francophone African states. This programme, which has since been established on a sound footing and is now as important as that to Commonwealth African

---

[3] A French Canadian despite his name.

states, had a complex mixture of motives: a recognition of the need to find an outlet for French-speaking Canadians, the aid effort previously having been almost exclusively Commonwealth-oriented; a determination to pre-empt a Quebec aid programme in Africa, of which signs were beginning in the late 1960s; and a political recognition that the next stage of the battle over Quebec's international personality would be fought in Africa and that an effective aid programme would strengthen Ottawa's armoury. But, while the first small allocation had been made in 1961 and thereafter steadily increased, almost no projects had been approved. To overcome these embarrassing delays, the Pearson government in 1968 sent an ex-cabinet minister on a whirlwind tour of the continent with authority to make commitments without reference to Ottawa.

French Africa did prove to be the next battleground. Canada participated in the two francophone conferences at Niamey, the capital of Niger, in 1969 and 1970, at which an association of French-language states concerned with cultural and technical co-operation (l'Agence de Coopération culturelle et technique) was set up. This provoked a rivalry between Ottawa and Quebec which was considered to have fundamental implications—whether the province of Quebec could be recognized as a fully fledged member-state in the organization. A certain confusion on the part of newly independent African states can be explained by their unfamiliarity with Canada and their lack of understanding and experience of the constitutional structure of federal states. But no such excuses can be given for the behind-the-scenes encouragement and even sponsorship by the French of what was in fact an effort to have Quebec accorded some kind of international recognition as a sovereign state. To protest the invitation extended to the Quebec government to attend a conference of francophone education ministers in Libreville, capital of Gabon, the Canadian government had felt it necessary in March 1968 to announce that it had instructed its ambassador-designate to Gabon not to present his credentials—in effect pointedly deferring the establishment of diplomatic relations.

The struggle over international recognition obscured a genuine problem. L'Agence de Coopération culturelle et technique

and the conferences of education ministers were of significance
to French-speaking Canadians and it was necessary to
work out a formula for effectively representing the Quebec
government in their work, which concerned education and cultural exchanges, spheres of government activity reserved for the
provinces under the Canadian constitution. As long as Quebec
and Ottawa were in conflict over representation in the Agency
and at educational conferences, the real problem was ignored.
The challenge was clearly presented by Paul Gérin-Lajoie, then
Quebec minister of education, now president of the federal
Canadian International Development Agency, in a statement
made to the consular corps in Montreal in 1964:

Dans une fédération comme le Canada, il est maintenant nécessaire
que les collectivités-membres qui le désirent, participent activement
et directement à l'élaboration des conventions internationales qui
les intéressent. . . . Il n'est plus admissible que l'Etat fédéral puisse
exercer une sorte de surveillance et de contrôle d'opportunité sur les
relations internationales du Québec.[4]

It is a sign of the cooling of tension and of genuine progress
made that Canada was represented at the 1970 conference in
Niamey, the capital of Niger, at which the Agency was formally
inaugurated, by a single delegation comprising federal representatives and representatives from four provinces with sizeable
French Canadian populations: Quebec, New Brunswick,
Ontario, and Manitoba. The special position of the provinces,
of importance particularly to Quebec, was recognized by
according to the representatives of each province the right to
express their own viewpoint. While the formula for joint representation is vague and deliberately ambiguous, it is now accepted
that generally in areas of provincial legislative competence, the
delegation will abstain unless the provincial representatives are
unanimous. These arrangements were taken one stage further
when the Agency held a regular meeting in Ottawa and Quebec
in October 1971. Terms and conditions were worked out under
which Quebec was admitted as a ' participating government to
the institutions, activities and programs of the Agency ',[5] thereby

---

[4] As quoted in L. Sabourin, ' Politique étrangère et " Etat du Québec " ',
Internat. J., Summer 1965, p. 350.
[5] Dept. of External Affairs, communiqué ' Modalities according to which the

making an important step towards according Quebec recognition of the distinct identity to which it aspires. The federal government could at the same time derive satisfaction from the fact that:

En tenant chez nous sa première assemblée complète et réguliére, l'Agence et avec elle, la francophonie, déjà européenne, africaine et asiatique, se reconnaissent une fois pour toutes et un avenir et un partenaire en Amérique. Le terme de ' francophonie ' dit parfaitement le bien qui nous unit: une langue commune, le français[6]

in the words of Trudeau addressing the Ottawa conference of the Agency.

The major concerns of both Ottawa and Quebec have thus been satisfied. However, the arrangements for voting are ambiguous and could lead to new problems, given the extreme sensitivity of the complex arrangements. But in the meantime the Agency and several other institutions spanning the francophone world have been established and it is now reasonable to compare this structure with that of the Commonwealth. The main difference is that the francophone community comprehends states—notably Belgium, Canada, and the Zaire Republic (Congo/Kinshasa)—deriving from empires other than that of France. Accordingly the francophone world has neither sought nor attained the same sense of community at the level of head of government; there are no conferences of prime ministers. Emphasis has been deliberately placed on the functional level—education, technical co-operation, economic assistance, cultural contacts—and structures are being built where no previous ties existed. It is a comment on the central position which Canada has been able to acquire in the francophone community, as in the Commonwealth, that Canadians head the main co-operative structures in both organizations: Jean-Marc Léger being secrétaire général of the Agency and Arnold Smith heading the Commonwealth Secretariat.

Although Africa was the scene of much skirmishing, Ottawa

government of Quebec is admitted as a participating government to the institutions, activities and programs of the Agency for Cultural and Technical Co-operation as agreed on October 1, 1971, between the government of Canada and the government of Quebec ', 8 Oct. 1971.
[6] Office of PM, press release, 11 Oct. 1971.

regarded France as the only adversary in this conflict. The evolution in the French attitude in the 1960s reflected the mutations of General de Gaulle's own approach. While visiting Canada in 1960, he had displayed the traditional French hauteur toward Quebec and French Canadians. But the Quiet Revolution and the evident need of French Canadians for cultural support from France had caught his imagination. Responding to Premier Lesage's overtures, France had initiated important programmes in the field of education and technical training in the French language. An intergovernmental commission was established and in 1965 the offices of the Quebec representative in France were greatly expanded and placed under the direction of a former federal ambassador. France subsequently enlarged its consulate in Quebec City to become a major point of contact.

Disquiet in Ottawa turned to anxiety as President de Gaulle began to receive each visiting Quebec minister, while visits of federal ministers were virtually ignored and the Canadian ambassador, after presenting his credentials in 1964, was not again received in audience by the president. The visit of Premier Johnson in May 1967 marked a new level of provocation when the only flags displayed were those of France and Quebec. The climax came with General de Gaulle's visit to Canada in July 1967, the centennial year. Insisting on beginning his journey in Quebec City rather than Ottawa, he staged a triumphant progress from Quebec to Montreal along the old Chemin du Roy, which reminded him, as he provocatively stated later, of the wartime liberation atmosphere. In Montreal on the balcony of the Hôtel de Ville, before a vast crowd, he pronounced his famous statement, the motto of Quebec separatists, ' Vive le Québec libre! '. Informed by the prime minister, Pearson, that his statements were ' unacceptable to the Canadian people and its Government ', he called off his visit to Ottawa and returned dramatically to France.

In spite of the apparent community of interest between President de Gaulle and the Quebec separatists, there was and remains in fact a drastic difference in perception. De Gaulle's approach remained essentially that of a French nationalist patriarch. At his first press conference following his visit to

Quebec, he spoke of ' la volonté des Français [by which he meant French Canadians] de prendre en main leurs affaires. . . . ils considèrent la mère patrie non plus seulement comme un souvenir très cher, mais comme la nation dont le sang, le coeur, l'esprit sont les mêmes que les leurs '.[7] Separatists never refer to themselves as French or French Canadians but always as Québécois. They are Quebec nationalists, naturally ready to exploit any source of possible support, and particularly one as powerful and dedicated as General de Gaulle.

Following this visit, and as long as de Gaulle remained president, official Franco-Canadian relations were troubled and bitter; some major confrontations at several conferences in Africa have already been noted. Nevertheless the Pearson and Trudeau governments deliberately sought to maintain contacts in areas of practical activity: an agreement on co-operation in military research and development was negotiated and the cultural agreement continued to function. Since 1969 several developments have restored relations to a normal, and even a cordial, basis. The most important of these was the accession of President Pompidou. He has moved slowly but steadily to end provocations and to introduce normalcy in the relationship, while taking care never to give his Gaullist supporters clear evidence of a change in policy. This was a delicate task in the period of transition when the operating principles of French policy remained those formulated by de Gaulle. The visit of the French secretary of state for foreign affairs, Jean de Lipkowski, in October 1969 is an excellent illustration. He had been the prime executor in the Quai d'Orsay of de Gaulle's policy of snubbing Ottawa, and his visit in 1969 was to Quebec alone. Pressed by the federal government to stop over in Ottawa, he declined on the ground that his timetable would not permit it, and then in Quebec City made a provocative public statement about the Canadian constitution. This incident, and some French manoeuvres at the 2nd Niamey conference a few months later, aroused suspicions—an instinctive response in Ottawa at the time—that Pompidou was following faithfully in the footsteps of de Gaulle. Over time, confidence in the good faith of President Pompidou has been gradually established. However,

[7] Charles de Gaulle, press conference, Paris, 27 Nov. 1967.

the fear remains that French officials are not all to be trusted to follow his directives, and it is appreciated that the president has to move with a certain caution.

President Pompidou's policy was aided by several developments which defused the competition between Ottawa and Quebec: the election in 1968 of a federal Liberal government headed by a Quebecker, Pierre Trudeau, and, more significantly, the unexpected triumph of Robert Bourassa and the Quebec Liberal party in April 1970 on an avowedly federalist platform. Premier Bourassa has put the accent on building up the Quebec economy and has consciously played down the provocative aspects of Quebec's foreign activities. These electoral results and, subsequently, the total defeat of the nationalists in the Montreal municipal elections by Mayor Drapeau's party, admittedly in the emotional atmosphere of the Cross kidnapping, have forced French authorities to recognize that Quebec's separation may not be inevitable and that prudence dictates a more detached attitude to Canada. Another reason for caution is the recognition that France does not have the economic strength to lend support to an independent Quebec, should separation occur. Indeed, efforts in recent years to encourage French investment in Quebec have been spectacularly unsuccessful; much of the French investment made in the last fifteen years has been in other parts of Canada.

The treatment of Premier Bourassa's formal visit to France in April 1971 was impeccable in the view of the federal authorities. The next step was the visit by Maurice Schumann, the French foreign minister, to Ottawa on 22 September, followed a week later by an equally short visit to Quebec City. All that remains for the restoration of formal cordiality is a successful visit by Trudeau to France, although Pompidou has not yet decided to extend the necessary invitation. Even after that, it will still take some time to overcome memories of the past.

Within Canada and abroad there is a tendency to attribute the trouble between Ottawa and Quebec to de Gaulle's interference. He was indeed a serious irritant, but an underlying tension exists which derives from forces of history acting on the peculiar relationships which prevail within Canada. One important factor has been the UN itself. During the 1960s

Quebeckers have watched the attainment of independence with UN encouragement by more than two score states. By comparison with Quebec, almost all of them are physically and and demographically smaller, in the main less well endowed with natural resources, far less industrialized, and lacking a well educated population with a strong consciousness of a historically based nationality. These factors, dramatized by the appearance of the leaders of these new countries on the UN rostrum in New York a few hundred miles from Montreal, have called into question the conviction which used to be generally accepted that God and history had decreed that French Canadians should be a minority in English-speaking Canada. Now French Canadian nationalists can point to these newly independent states and say: ' If they, why not we? '

This new and powerful argument has presented itself at a moment in history when uncertain forces are stimulating a revival of other culturally distinct nationalisms such as the Scots, the Welsh, the Bretons, and the Basques. For these peoples this return to cultural roots may be an instinctive response to the diminished significance of loyalty to the nation state in a continent which has suffered two world wars and which is now moving towards continental integration. It is none the less an encouragement to French Canadians, whose sense of community has undoubtedly been stimulated further through the medium of television.

Minority or resistance movements elsewhere have also had their effects on the political violence in Quebec. Quebeckers have been arrested working with black resistance groups in New York, have trained with the Palestine guerrillas in Jordan, and have reportedly sought training and indoctrination in Cuba and Algeria. Many of the demands and the publicity techniques of the terrorists used during the kidnapping crisis of the autumn of 1970 were taken direct from Latin American terrorist activities. FLQ (Front de Libération de Québec) members see themselves as part of a world-wide movement.

The impact of all these developments on Canadian foreign policy is hard to exaggerate. The deterioration in relations with France, only now returning to normal; the establishment of diplomatic relations with a number of French African states, including the opening of several resident missions,[8] and the effort spent in cultivating these states; the mounting of a large aid programme in francophone Africa; active Canadian participation in l'Agence de Coopération culturelle et technique and in l'Association des universités partiellement et entièrement de langue française (AUPELF); membership in l'Association des parlementaires de langue française is part of an effort, which the government judges to be successful, to have Canada ' accepted internationally as being equally a French-speaking and an English-speaking country '.[9] The development of a doctrine of co-operative federalism abroad, including more satisfactory arrangements for including provincial representatives on Canadian delegations; the advocacy of increased use of French at the UN—all these steps represent a significant shift of emphasis and resources and are all attributable to the events of the last decade in Quebec. These are, however, only outward manifestations. They do not reveal the extent to which these problems have preoccupied the higher levels of the Department of External Affairs and the prime minister and other ministers directly affected, the number of crises which have sapped the energy and used up the time of ministers, with sometimes the only evidence for their effort being the avoidance of crisis.

Other regional strains

Although the Quebec question is more dramatic, other areas of federal-provincial relations are also under increased strain. The size of the country and the clashing regional interests make this inevitable. Under the Canadian constitution the larger share of the revenues is collected by the federal government and then redistributed, according to very complex formulas, to the provinces. In recent years the rapid growth in the costs of education (entirely under provincial jurisdiction) and of social welfare (largely under provincial jurisdiction) has been a constant cause of tension. Thus in the period 1954–64 provincial and municipal spending increased by 206 per cent while

[8] In 1971 Canada had missions in six French-speaking African states, Algeria, Cameroon, Côte d'Ivoire, Zaïre (Congo-Kinshasa), Senegal, Tunisia, as compared with four Commonwealth English-speaking states, Ghana, Kenya, Nigeria, and Tanzania.

[9] Secretary of State for External Affairs, SCEAND *Mins. of Proc. & Evidence*, 19 May 1971, p. 27-8.

that of the federal government increased by only 56 per cent.[10] With shifts in expenditure of this order of magnitude, it is no wonder that conflict between the two levels of government has intensified. Apart from absorbing the time and energy of both federal and provincial cabinets, this development increases the pressure for reducing major external expenditures such as defence. Trudeau specifically noted in a speech in Calgary on 12 April 1969: ' There is a tendency in the past few years . . . on the part of provincial governments, to say to the federal government: " Spend less on defence and you'll have more for . . . other worthwhile project[s]." '

Constitutional issues and international problems have been rubbing against one another in a further respect in recent years. Increasingly, as a result of the expanded role of governments, many areas of policy which in Canada come under the jurisdiction of the provinces have become the subject of international negotiation and agreement. In the past, although Canadian provinces and adjoining American states have entered into agreements which may have been, strictly speaking, international, these implications were ignored. The federal government has either chosen to regard them as ' arrangements subsumed under agreements between Canada and foreign governments concerned ' or as ' administrative arrangements of an informal character . . . not subject to international law '.[11] Likewise many of the provinces have maintained offices abroad, mostly in London or in New York, to promote provincial exports, attract investment, and encourage tourism. This too was ignored. However, once France began a conscious policy of building up Quebec's international personality, the sovereignty of the federal state was involved and the issue could no longer be overlooked. Inevitably, but nevertheless regrettably, a double standard developed. Comparable actions by Quebec and by English-speaking provinces were judged differently. In the atmosphere of supicion which flourished, foreign aid offered by Ontario directly to the countries of the Caribbean was welcomed in Ottawa, whereas Quebec's early efforts in the French

[10] Gilles Boyer in *Le Soleill*, quoted in *Globe and Mail*, 23 June 1971.

[11] Canada, White Paper, *Federalism and International Relations* (1968), p. 26.

African states were seen as competition with Ottawa—which it undeniably was.

The traditional concept of sovereignty was developed before federal states emerged, and federal states preserved at the time of their founding the indivisible character of sovereignty by reserving foreign affairs wholly to the federal government. But the widened scope of intergovernmental relations has brought into the sphere of inter-state dealings areas of policy which fall within provincial jurisdiction. Until the problem with Quebec arose the federal government was responding rather grudgingly to the need for provincial representation in delegations at conferences dealing with subjects within provincial competence. The administrative complications are admittedly considerable. With ten provinces varying enormously in size and wealth, ranging from Ontario's population of almost seven million to Prince Edward Island's 108, 535,[12] how are delegations to be selected? How do they reach agreement? The general practice in the past had been for the federal government to negotiate conventions in areas which concerned the provinces, consulting as it considered necessary; it then reserved Canada's position to determine how the provinces responded and finally ratified the convention only if the provinces all signified their approval. This process is time-consuming and cumbersome and the results often unsatisfactory. For example, Canada has to date ratified only one of the four UN Conventions on Human Rights because one province has not signified its approval of the other three.

The tensions with France of the last decade have created a considerable change in outlook. The initial response was one of ultra-sensitivity, and in moments of crisis the federal government sought to assert its constitutional rights. But underlying the rivalry was a genuine problem, and fortunately it has proven possible gradually to work out arrangements which respect the position of the federal government while providing for the legitimate interests of the provinces, and of Quebec in particular. On the basis of theoretical work elaborated in two White Papers of 1968, *Federalism and International Relations* and *Federalism and International Conferences on Education*, and in counter-submissions by the provinces, particularly by Ontario and

[12] *Canada Year Book, 1968*. Figures are for 1966.

Quebec, to the continuing constitutional conferences, ' ad hoc ' arrangements are being worked out for joint federal-provincial representation at international meetings in which the provinces have an interest. The formulas devised for francophone conferences have already been fully discussed, but it is equally significant that the delegation to the preparatory meeting in February 1971 for the Stockholm Conference on the Environment had eighteen provincial representatives. Parallel to these developments, the Department of External Affairs in its latest reorganization has a strengthened Co-ordination Bureau bringing together the several divisions established during the last decade with responsibilities in this politically sensitive area of policy.

This is complex innovative work. Even in the field of representation where the most effort has been made, new problems constantly arise. Thus, Premier Lougheed, elected in the autumn of 1971 to head a conservative government in the province of Alberta, the principal Canadian source of oil and gas, announced his government's intention of opening a mission in Washington to promote and protect Albertan interests in the energy field and asserted that Alberta should ' have an official observer, of our choosing, sitting there at the discussion—be they at the ministerial level or at the official level between Canada and the United States—if energy is to be one of the major subjects discussed '.[13]

In responding to these pressures and in enlarging the circle of consultation, the federal authorities are voluntarily increasing the problem of elaborating policy. The practice to date is still rather rudimentary. For example, the whole field of information distribution has scarcely been touched; that is, reports received from the Canadian embassies abroad are not normally and automatically distributed to the interested provinces, even when they concern matters of particular interest to the provinces such as the development of markets abroad for agricultural products. But a beginning has been made in involving the provinces in foreign activity and this could become an important Canadian contribution to the practice of international affairs.

[13] *Globe and Mail*, 8 Nov. 1971.

To a foreign observer the provincial sorties into international affairs and the federal response appear quite unusual. An American commentator has concluded that: ' The Canadian provincial governments will continue to press for and to exercise foreign powers unthinkable in the American, Mexican or Brazilian state contexts. These powers will sooner or later become articulated and entrenched in the proposed Canadian constitution.'[14] However, to a thoughtful Quebec academic, Professor Maurice Torrelli, these developments appeared to go some way to resolving a basic problem:

D'une part, en effet, le Canada se trouve enfermé dans le dilemme classique de l'Etat fédéral: les autorités fédérales ont le pouvoir de conclure des traités mais le Parlement du Canada n'est pas habilité à adopter la législation mettant en oeuvre ces traités lorsque leur objet relève de la compétence provinciale; les provinces ont la compétence législative dans certains domaines mais elles n'ont pas le pouvoir de conclure des accords internationaux. . . .

D'autre part, l'apparition de nouveaux besoins, le développement des relations internationales, la volonté de faire respecter les particularismes face à des interdépendences économiques, socio-culturelles accrues, incitent de plus en plus à reconnaître la légitimité des aspirations d'un Etat comme le Québec à participer à la vie internationale . . . Dans cette perspective, les propositions présentées par le gouvernement fédéral dans le cadre de la révision constitutionelle portent la marque d'un effort intéressant en vue d'assurer un fédéralisme concerté ou coopératif dans le domaine des relations extérieures.[15]

Another development with interesting constitutional implications relates to foreign visits by the Governor-General of Canada. Legally speaking, Queen Elizabeth is the Canadian head of state, and the Governor-General has only vice-regal status. While Georges Vanier, a long-time friend of President de Gaulle, was Governor-General in the mid-1960s, it was felt that a visit by Vanier to Paris might help to improve Franco-Canadian relations. However, de Gaulle insisted that Vanier would not be accorded head-of-state treatment and the visit

[14] G. Rutan, ' Provincial participation in Canadian foreign relations ', *J. Inter-Amer. Stud. & World Affairs*, Apr. 1971, p. 244.

[15] M. Torrelli, ' Les relations extérieures du Québec ', *Ann. français de Droit int.*, *1970*, pp. 202–3.

was never arranged. The present Governor-General, Roland Michener, has already undertaken three visits where he was received as Canadian head of state, to Trinidad and Guyana in 1969 and to the Benelux countries in 1971. With the attendance of the Governor-General at the Iranian ceremony in honour of the 2,500th anniversary of the founding of the Persian Empire in October 1971, this careful programme to gain international recognition of the Governor-General as ' de facto ' head of state is now quite far advanced.

This discussion by no means exhausts the list of constitutional issues now under review in Canada, although it does cover those with direct foreign policy implications. The whole process of preparation and participation in the now-frequent constitutional conferences is enormously time-consuming. The main impact is the absorption of much of the cabinet's time. Cabinet is at the best of times the bottleneck in processing government business. Léo Cadieux, when he was minister of defence, replied to a question concerning the delay in cabinet decision-making on a major issue. The problem, he said, was ' simply getting it onto the Cabinet agenda '.[16]

Such time as has been available for foreign affairs has usually been taken up dealing with crises, of which the kidnapping of James Cross in the autumn of 1970 was the supreme example. This pre-empted the time of parliament and cabinet for a couple of months. It also involved the Department of External Affairs. Because Cross was a diplomat, the Department was involved from the outset and its operations room became the government's nerve centre. When Pierre Laporte was kidnapped, no changes in organizational arrangements were made. During the whole autumn, the under-secretary and a staff in his office were occupied, at times for more than twenty hours a day, in coping exclusively with the implications of the kidnappings, with the natural consequence that other interests and initiatives were largely ignored. Of all the strains caused by the constitutional and related problems of the past few years, this was probably the greatest on the time of ministers and cabinet.

[16] *Globe and Mail,* 11 Mar. 1970.

5

CONTINENTAL DRIFT OR CONTINENTAL DIVIDE?

SINCE Confederation in 1867, which created the Dominion of Canada, indeed even before, the only serious external challenge to Canada's survival as an independent entity has come from the south. In spite of strong pressure at various times, and especially in the nineteenth century when the United States was driven by a sense of Manifest Destiny to gain control of the whole continent, only one war was fought—in 1812. By 1817 a successful disarmament agreement, known as the Rush–Bagot Agreement, ended naval rivalry on the Great Lakes. Then, as the great westward trek of European immigrants got under way, first in the United States and later in Canada, the major boundary disputes were resolved, and although at the time there were many charges of British sell-outs, these border settlements have not been called into question. With their conclusion, disputes between the two governments over territory ceased to be a source of conflict. And in succeeding years a number of joint Canada-US institutions were set up to resolve points of difference amicably.

Physical conflict at the inter-state level having been resolved, there was a period during the 1850s and 1860s when the Fenians, a kind of early and ineffective IRA, carried out raids which became a major irritant to good relations and played some part in the movement for confederation in the Canadian colonies. Increasingly, however, the American challenge was seen in economic terms. Canada, from the first, has had a narrow band of settled territory crowding the border with the United States. Ninety per cent of Canadians live within 200 miles of this over 4,000-mile border. North-south movement was natural, and even encouraged by geographical links such as the Red River valley connecting Winnipeg and St Paul-Minneapolis, but it threatened the break-up of the country. The response of Canadian governments in the late nineteenth century was the building of the transcontinental railway line to provide an east-west link and a high-tariff policy to protect Canadian industry from cheaper large-scale US production. In political terms, this view was advocated by the Canada First movement founded in the early 1870s. In their pamphlet of 1871 entitled *Canada First or Our New Nationality*, it was pointed out that ' as between the various Provinces comprising the Dominion, we need some cement more binding than geographical contact; some bond more uniting than a shiftless expediency; some lode-star more potent than a mere community of profit . . . '.[1]

The impulse for this kind of early nationalism was to protect Canada from absorption by the United States. The inevitability of such a development has always had its soothsayers, and even its advocates. An early and highly cultivated British emigrant to Canada, Goldwin Smith, speaking in 1866, affirmed:

Grow the American Federation must. . . . But the growth will be that of peaceful expansion and attraction, not of forcible annexation. . . . The British North American colonies will in time, and probably at no very distant time, unite themselves politically to the Group of States, of which they are already by race, position, commercial ties and the characteristics of their institutions a part.[2]

The paradox in Canada's relations with the United States is that, even while the primary challenge to national survival is seen as some kind of absorption by the United States, the two countries probably enjoy closer and more intimate relations than do any other countries of the world. Trade between them has reached astonishing proportions: almost 70 per cent of Canadian trade is with the United States, and even for the United States, trade with Canada represents 26 per cent of its world-wide total. US trade with Canada ($19,528 million in 1969) is almost equal to its trade with the EEC and the UK combined ($20,702 million in 1969).[3] Thirty per cent of all US foreign investment is in Canada, yet the per capita Canadian investment in the United States is 50 per cent greater than per capita American investment in Canada. Over 1,300,000 Canadian workers belong to ' international unions ', the vast majority of which

[1] Quoted in D. G. Creighton, *Dominion of the North* (Cambridge, Mass., 1944), p. 322.
[2] Quoted in J. Willison, *Reminiscences, Political and Personal* (Toronto, 1919), p. 73.
[3] US Dept. of State, *US Foreign Policy 1969–70* (1971), p. 190.

have US headquarters.[4] Canadian-American links in everything from professional associations to protest groups are intimate and regular. There are over thirty-five million visits by
Canadians to the United States each year and an even greater
number of Americans cross the border annually into
Canada.

How is it, with the unequalled range of relationships between
the two countries, that Canada was ignored in President Nixon's
two major reports of February 1970 and February 1971, entitled
US Foreign Policy for the 1970s? Canadians were quick to notice
not only this omission, but that the section on the western hemisphere began with a reference to sister republics, thereby indi-
cating that even subconsciously Canada was being ignored. The
explanation is, of course, that Americans in general and even
the government look on Canada, not as a foreign nation, but
rather as a kind of relative with whom they share common
domestic problems. While this habit of mind is irritating to
many Canadians, it is of immense importance for the maintenance of Canada's unique relationship with its neighbour.

For Canadians the distortion is just as extreme—and leads at
times to some curiously parallel results. Obviously relations with
the United States are the overriding concern at every level of
Canadian foreign policy. Yet *Foreign Policy for Canadians* failed to
deal with the United States, apart from a number of general
observations. This omission, while seemingly illogical, can be
explained nonetheless by the complications and intricacies
facing the formulators of a complete and consistent Canadian
policy towards the United States. It is difficult to think of any
major area of Canadian domestic policy—trade, finance, transport, communication, energy sources, defence, water, fisheries,
agriculture—where the impact and interests of the United
States are not of vital importance. The relationship is not only
more intricate than that between any other two countries in the
world, but the disproportionate power of the two countries
causes further complications. As the prime minister observed
before the National Press Club in Washington on 25 March
1969, ' Living next to you is in some ways like sleeping with an

[4] Dom. Bureau Statist., Report on *Labour Unions* under the Corporations and
Labour Unions Returns Act (CALURA), (1967), p. 37.

elephant. No matter how friendly and even-tempered is the beast, one is affected by every twitch and grunt.'

Economic relations

The Trudeau government, like its predecessors, has preferred to attack the problem of formulating its policy towards the United States on a piecemeal basis, dealing with various areas separately. To study the question of foreign ownership—a subject on which there has been considerable public pressure— a task force [5] under the personal direction of a cabinet minister, Herb Gray, was set up in March 1970. This had proved so complex a study that a year and a half later it was still not complete. Moreover, the uncertainty caused by President Nixon's 15 August 1971 crash programme for overcoming the US balance-of-payments deficit may force the Trudeau government to reconsider some of the tentative decisions it had already taken. If the DISC (Domestic International Sales Corporation) legislation is approved by Congress, Canada may even be faced with a sharp decline in American investment, a contingency which would present the Canadian government with an entirely new situation.

Canada, as a developing country, has always been a large importer of capital. Until World War I, the principal source was the United Kingdom, and it came mainly in the form of debt capital. Large-scale American investment began in the interwar period through the establishment of wholly-owned subsidiaries to exploit the Canadian market and in many instances to profit from preferred access to a wider market represented by the imperial preference system adopted in 1932. The close cultural links between the two countries have made it easier for US companies to sell their products in Canada; since Canadians buy US periodicals and listen to US radio and television programmes, advertising campaigns intended to blanket US audiences generally cover a large number of Canadians at no extra cost.

[5] The Pearson government had earlier set up a task force to study this same problem. The report, *Foreign Ownership and the Structure of Canadian Industry* presented in January 1968, documented the consequences of foreign ownership and investment to Canada and prescribed certain policies. The government neither accepted nor rejected the report, which nevertheless became an important document in a mounting public discussion.

The dominating position of US investment in the Canadian economy occurred after World War II. On the one hand Britain was obliged to liquidate a number of its investments to purchase munitions in Canada; on the other, as the United States began to experience shortages of raw materials, it turned naturally to develop those resources which were often in large supply in its neighbour to the north. More often than not this was done by direct investment, with the initiative, the capital, the technology, and frequently even the management coming from the United States. In manufacturing, the growth of the multinational firm was reflected in a continuing series of mergers and direct sales.

Canada has moved slowly to dam this flood. The need for capital, jobs, technology, and markets has inclined governments at the federal and even more at the provincial levels to encourage foreign investment. In the last few years some European and Japanese investment interest has developed, but the United States remains and undoubtedly will remain by far the predominant source. Canada has fewer controls on foreign investment than any other advanced industrial country in the world. Such controls as have been applied were intended only to exclude foreign investment from certain key sectors of the economy. A variety of techniques has been used: placing low upper limits on the ownership of the equity of firms engaged in certain businesses such as banking, television, and broadcasting, and federally incorporated trust, loan, sales, finance, and life insurance companies; withholding tax advantages such as the right to deduct expenses for advertising if placed in non-Canadian periodicals;[6] using the power of national licensing or regulatory bodies, such as the Canadian Transport Commission and the National Energy Board, to set rates and conditions of operations in industries considered of prime national importance. An additional important technique for ensuring Canadian ownership has been actual public ownership or participation, for example in airlines, railway transport, atomic energy,

---

[6] *Time* and *Readers Digest*, which print slightly modified editions for the Canadian market, have been especially exempted and are regarded as Canadian periodicals for this purpose. This exceptional treatment has been a source of irritation to many Canadians.

uranium processing, oil exploration in the Arctic, and synthetic rubber production.[7]

These devices have created certain islands of Canadian investment, but the flood of US investment surges around them. The following table indicates the growth of US investment, compared with that of Britain and others (principally other European countries and lately Japan). Over 80 per cent of all non-resident direct investment in Canada now comes from the United States.

Direct investment (book value) in Canada
($ million)

Year	US	UK	Other
1936	1,952		
1946	2,428	335	63
1956	7,392	1,048	428
1965	13,940	2,013	1,255
1967	17,000	2,152	1,547
1969	21,075*		

* US dollars.

Sources: *Canada Year Book 1942*; Dept. of Ind., Trade & Commerce, *Foreign Direct Investment in Canada since the Second World War* (1970); US Dept of Commerce, *Survey of Current Business*, Oct. 1970, p. 23; *Statistics Canada*, Dec. 1971.

Perhaps even more significant than the amount of US direct investment is the control which this investment represents and the value of the assets of US-controlled corporations in Canada, shown in the table on p. 62. A foreign owner may often exercise control through a concentrated holding which represents substantially less than 50 per cent of the corporate assets of the company. The actual value of the assets of US-controlled corporations in Canada was estimated by a government study in 1968 to be over $35 billion out of total Canadian corporate assets of $190 billion.[8]

[7] A wartime anomaly which has prospered.
[8] 1968 Report under CALURA, p. 176.

Assets of corporations by country in which control is held,
1968 figures (per cent)

Industry	US	UK	Other	Total foreign	Canada
Mining					
metal	37·6	1·7	12·4	51·7	46·6*
mineral fuels	67·1	5·4	10·6	83·1	16·4
other	41·9	4·1	13·6	59·6	33·5
Selected manufacturing					
rubber products	84·0	...	...	93·1	6·1
machinery	64·8	3·7	3·6	72·1	25·5
transport equipment	73·2	13·6	·2	87·0	12·2
electrical products	58·1	3·7	2·1	63·9	31·7
petroleum & coal products	76·4	...	...	99·7	·2
chemicals & chemical products	56·6	21·1	3·8	81·5	11·5

* totals do not equal 100 per cent due to non-reporting corporations.
... not available.

Source: Dom. Bureau Statist., Report on *Corporations* under Corporations and Labour Unions Returns Act (1968), p. 177.

It should be evident to Europeans that this situation is a disturbing one. Europeans have themselves begun to react to large-scale US investments; indeed, during the last decade, US investment in Western Europe in absolute terms grew faster than it did in Canada, to the point where US direct investment in 1969 amounted to some $21 billion.[9] As in Canada, this investment tends to be concentrated in the fastest growing areas of the economy. The degree of European concern has been attested by the instant and continuing success of Servan-Schreiber's *Le Défi américain*. But compare this situation with that in Canada. In Europe, an investment of $21 billion is spread over 300 millions of people, divided among more than a dozen countries with distinct and historic cultures. In Canada, $21 billion is spread over twenty-one millions of peoples, two-thirds

[9] US Dept. of Commerce, *Survey of Current Business*, Oct. 1970, p. 28.

of whom are culturally akin to Americans and who in the main share the same cultural fare.

These facts account for the growth of a widespread concern in Canada over their implications for Canada's future independence. It is not that the US government has been using this power to intervene in Canadian affairs; the investment is private and diffuse, and the United States has no interest in absorbing or taking over Canada. There are some specific Canadian complaints about the extraterritorial application of US anti-trust laws and of its Trading with the Enemy Act, and concern about distortions caused within the economy and about the implications of the development of the multinational corporation, but the most important threat has been to Canadian self-confidence. In the absence of an explicit policy on foreign investment, the Trudeau government felt it necessary—for the first time in Canadian history—to move arbitrarily to block the sale to US interests of a large uranium producer in 1970 and of the largest remaining independent Canadian oil company in 1971. In the meantime, the government's freedom of manoeuvre is tempered by the high level of unemployment (reaching 8·1 per cent of the labour force during the winter of 1970–1), the more so because this unemployment is concentrated in certain regions of the country, including the politically sensitive province of Quebec, where unemployment amounted to 10·4 per cent during the same period.[10] Most provincial governments have therefore been vociferous, publicly and privately, in opposing any measure which might reduce the flow of foreign investment.

A variety of pressure groups has recently been formed to press for more rapid and vigorous action by the federal government to limit future US investment and even to roll it back. One of the more active, known as the Waffle group, is attempting, by working from within it, to radicalize the policies of the New Democratic party, a socialist party forming the second strongest opposition group in the House. The largest organization, the Committee for an Independent Canada, set up in 1970, is urging the government to increase the proportion of Canadian ownership of the economy, through various techniques such as tax incentives, tax penalties, the establishment of a federal agency

[10] Dom. Bureau Statist., *Monthly Labour Force* (1971), Table 1, 8.

to supervise the conduct of foreign-controlled operations in Canada, and an agency to review or supervise any new take-overs. It is headed by an influential group of men including a former Liberal minister of finance, Walter Gordon, and a former Conservative national organizer, Edwin Goodman. Its formation is symptomatic of a growing, yet still rather diffuse, state of national alarm over the potential threat to independence represented by this mass of strategically-placed private American investment.

In November 1971 several concerned Toronto academics took matters into their own hands and, in an apparent attempt to force a government decision, published a ' draft ' of the still confidential report to the cabinet of the Gray task force on foreign ownership. The main recommendation was the establishment of a central screening agency to review foreign direct investment in Canada in order to maximize the benefits and reduce the disadvantages of such investment. A few days later a secret cabinet document revealing the government's agreement in principle to such a screening agency was published by a Montreal newspaper. The government has insisted that these decisions were subject to review pending further studies, but its freedom of manoeuvre has undoubtedly been limited.

Even if there has been no visible desire or attempt by the United States to exploit its potential economic power in Canada for political ends, many Canadians are worried about the consequences of this state of affairs. Some fear the development of a state of psychological subordination; others are afraid that emotional reactions will inhibit Canadians from co-operating in their own interest with Americans; while still others are concerned with the possible mortgaging of Canada's capacity for independent decision-making. This latter point alarmed the House of Commons Standing Committee on External Affairs and National Defence. Its 11th report on Canada–United States relations, prepared in 1970, concluded:

The danger facing Canada is not one of political absorption by the United States: the danger which Canada must guard against is that it will drift into such a position of dependency in relation to the United States that it will be unable, in practice, to adopt policies displeasing to the United States because of the fear of American reaction which would involve consequences unacceptable to Canadians (p. 13).

This concern is shared by the trade union movement. At the annual conference of the Canadian Labour Congress (CLC) in May 1970, the following resolution was passed:

WHEREAS there is a growing tendency toward a Canadian identity in the social and economic sectors of our society;

BE IT RESOLVED that the Canadian Labour Congress adopt a firm policy supporting minimum standards of self-government of the Canadian sections of international unions; and

BE IT FURTHER RESOLVED that these standards include: election of Canadian officers by Canadians; policies to deal with national affairs to be determined by the elected Canadian officers and/or members; Canadian elected representatives to have authority to speak for the union in Canada; and

BE IT FURTHER RESOLVED that the Canadian Labour Congress do all in its power to assist the affiliated unions in the attainment of these objectives.

Yet this same organization is composed of 117 separate unions, of which eighty-two are international unions, so called because they cover both the United States and Canada.[11] Inevitably the US section of each union is much more numerous and powerful (except for the International Woodworkers of America, and even its president is an American) and the Canadian part is normally treated as a regional component. These Canadian sections may have more or less practical autonomy, but the union headquarters are all in the United States and in law the power is often highly centralized. This state of legal dependency on the part of a large section of organized labour in Canada is disturbing and embarrassing to Canadian union leadership and rank and file alike. Yet the practical benefits remain attractive and the cost of separation high, so that the setting up of independent Canadian unions by members of international unions in Canada is unlikely. Instead there is pressure for greater autonomy. But the degree of progress is dependent very much on the attitude of the US leadership, because it is for each union to decide

[11] As n. 4, p. 58.

to what degree it is prepared to treat its Canadian section differently from regional sections in the United States.

The resulting slow progress towards union autonomy is frustrating and may lie in part behind the vigorously independent line on international questions which the CLC has been taking in recent years. Nowhere is this better illustrated than on the Vietnam question, where George Meany, president of the AFL-CIO, has supported the US administration's involvement while the CLC has been a strong critic of the whole enterprise. Arising out of this opposition to the Vietnam war, the CLC has called for ending the NORAD agreement and also the re-export by the United States to Vietnam of arms made in Canada, even though these steps could jeopardize the Defence Production Sharing Agreement with the United States. In general, therefore, and in marked and perhaps almost deliberate contrast with the AFL-CIO, the CLC has taken a more internationalist and idealistic approach to foreign policy.

Cultural dependency

The peculiar sensitivity of Canadians to the US economic role in Canada can only be understood if cultural relations between the two countries are also taken into account. In this respect, of course, French Canadians stand apart by reason of their separate language, even though they have assimilated much that is distinctly North American. The key is the cultural penetration of English-speaking Canada by the US media, particularly since the advent of television. Canadians have always read American periodicals, and only the fiscal penalties on advertising in non-Canadian periodicals have preserved a rather ailing native periodical press. Even so, distribution of periodical literature is largely in the hands of US-owned companies. Likewise government controls have preserved newspapers in Canadian hands, albeit in fewer and fewer hands and provided that Lord Thomson can be regarded as a Canadian. Nevertheless, for international news coverage and comment they rely heavily on the English-language international news services and on US syndicated columnists. Television and radio must also by law be owned and controlled by Canadians, but proximity to the border allows most Canadians to tune in directly on American programmes. The popularity of US productions has been a continuing challenge to Canadian producers, and again the government (through the Canadian Radio and Television Commission) had to step in and require that by October 1971 at least 50 per cent of all television and radio programmes must have direct Canadian content and by October 1972, at least 60 per cent. The sensitivity of Canadians can be judged from the outcry in northern cities too remote to receive television directly from the United States when their requests for authority to construct microwave cables to service local cablevision companies were refused by the Commission. The fact is that probably 25 per cent of all Canadians regularly watch US television stations, some of which in border areas have developed significant Canadian advertising revenue.

The list goes on indefinitely. Despite an international reputation as a maker of documentaries, Canadians have made almost no feature films, although a newly established government agency is now trying to encourage such a development. Most English- and even French-language books, including school texts, sold in Canada are published abroad or by foreign subsidiaries in Canada. It is estimated that Canadian firms have, at most, only 19 per cent of the dollar volume of book sales.[12] Restrictions on the import of books printed abroad into the United States and working agreements between publishers in the United States and Britain to share the world market have effectively limited Canadian publishers to the small Canadian market.

An area of recent preoccupation in the cultural field has been the increasing employment of Americans in the universities. The rapid growth of Canadian universities in the last decade, beyond Canada's own capacity to staff them, attracted many non-Canadian academics to Canadian universities. In 1970 nearly 40 per cent of all university teachers were non-Canadians (the foreign-born percentage would be much higher). Of these 10 per cent were British and 15 per cent Americans. In the social sciences and the humanities, the American proportion

[12] Donald Cameron, ' Jack McClelland and the crisis in Canadian publishing ', *Saturday Night* (Toronto), June 1971.

was 24 and 20 per cent respectively.[13] It is significant and typical that the British entrants arouse little concern and generally evoke gratitude. But the Americans are subject to all kinds of criticisms: that they recruit fellow Americans rather than Canadians; that they offer courses on American rather than Canadian subjects and encourage the use of US textbooks; that they bring in American vogues such as behaviourism; and that they encourage Canadian students to take sides on US internal problems such as Vietnam (since many of the American academics belong to the liberal opposition in the United States and have moved to Canada to escape Vietnam in one way or another). A lively debate within Canadian universities has been stimulated by what some regard as an American invasion, because over the years many Canadians have benefited from academic and sports scholarships offered by US universities. Indeed there has been a twelvefold growth in the numbers of Canadians studying in the United States since before the war. More significantly, of the 12,852 Canadians studying at universities in the United States in 1968–9, 5,168 were registered in graduate work.[14]

The issue has taken on a particular acerbity in the past year because for the first time Canada is producing an excess of graduates and postgraduates in many fields who are having difficulty in finding employment. Tension is therefore likely to remain high as long as this surplus persists. But while this may be a passing issue, at least in its present acute form, it well illustrates the unusual type of consideration that can affect the character of relations between the two countries.

In spite of the extraordinary cultural similarities and the continuing American impact, thinking Canadians are aware of important and growing differences. Unfortunately this is in part a matter of taking satisfaction from the misfortune of others. Canada has a small black population so that it escapes the whole range of interracial problems with which the United States is faced. Likewise, and in many ways linked to it, although the proportion of persons residing in rural areas is

---

[13] Dom. Bureau Statist., *Salaries and Qualifications of Teachers in Universities and Colleges in Canada* (1971).

[14] Dom. Bureau Statist., *Survey of Higher Education* (1968–9).

under 10 per cent in both countries, urban conglomeration and decay has gone much farther in the United States than in Canada. Finally, Canadians are grateful for having avoided the horror and the holocaust of the Vietnam war as well as the problems resulting from the drafting of hundreds of thousands of reluctant youths to fight. For these differences, most Canadians simply thank God.

Sovereignty in the Arctic

Public sensitivity can force a government to act whether it is ready to do so or not. Discovery of oil on the north slope of Alaska set in motion just such a chain of events in Canadian-American relations centering on the issue of sovereignty in the Arctic. Transportation of this oil to potential markets poses formidable technical obstacles. The Humble Oil Company of the United States decided to experiment with a supertanker converted into an icebreaker, the Manhattan. The shallowness of the Bering Strait precluded any approach from the Pacific. The alternative was the long northwest passage from Atlantic waters, commercially attractive because of the direct access it could offer to the populous east coast of the United States and to Europe. By the summer of 1969 Humble Oil was ready for its experiment, which began with the full support of the Canadian authorities, who provided navigational aid, special information on ice conditions, and the support ultimately of two icebreakers.

The slow passage of the Manhattan was followed by Canadians with the same interest as moon shots have evoked. But some members of the House of Commons Standing Committee on Indian Affairs and Northern Development were alarmed that the transit of the northwest passage might create an inter-nationally-accepted presumption that this ice-covered route was an international waterway. They were concerned, too, that Canadian claims to the land and the adjacent continental shelf in the northern archipelago might be contested if oil were to be found in quantity, which is geologically quite possible. So they pressed within the government for a reassertion of Canadian claims. This the government was reluctant to do, believing that Canadian ownership of the land and adjacent shelf could not be in doubt—in spite of the almost uninhabited character of the country—and contending that to assert a claim might call into question the already established legal position. This did not satisfy the small group of Liberal back-benchers, who decided to force the government's hand at the moment of the Manhattan's arrival in Arctic waters by asking for an emergency debate while a particularly contentious piece of legislation was being considered in the House. Eventually the prime minister personally had to meet these members and persuade them to refrain, presumably by offering to take action in the next session.

The Standing Committee kept up pressure, holding hearings and visiting the Arctic in the summer and overflying the Manhattan while it was traversing the passage. In the autumn they prepared a strongly argued report [15] which recommended ' . . . that the Government of Canada indicate to the world without delay, that vessels, surface and submarine, passing through Canada's Arctic Archipelago are and shall be subject to the sovereign control and regulation of Canada'. [16]

Throughout the autumn and winter the cabinet debated several possible approaches. Public interest continued, as the Manhattan prepared for a second voyage. The United States also embarked on a programme of building large Arctic icebreakers, its own having proved totally inadequate. All of this coincided with increasing public concern over the sale of Canadian enterprises to American companies. Even summer cottage owners began to complain that Americans were buying up all beach and lakefront land. The Arctic became a kind of test of Canada's resolve to hold on to its birthright.

[15] The committee members conceived of this report as a means of pressure to be exercised against the government, not as a specific prescription for action. The chairman, a Liberal, did not ask for concurrence of the House, the only method by which the government can in effect be asked to pronounce on a committee report. Traditionally the asking of concurrence had only been requested by the committee chairman, which had left the initiative on the government benches, but the opposition decided to test this convention and a Conservative member asked for concurrence. In a historic ruling, the Speaker decided that any member of the House could ask for concurrence. Although the government talked out the report (i.e., after the day's debate, under Canadian parliamentary rules, the item becomes government business), the opposition now had an issue and the public was by this time aroused. Clearly within the Liberal caucus there was also support for strong action.

[16] Parl., H. of C. Standing Committee on Indian Affairs & Northern Development, *1st Report* (16 Dec. 1969), p. 7.

By the spring of 1970 the cabinet had taken its tough decisions, and a series of measures with implications far beyond the Arctic were announced:

1. An amendment to the Territorial Sea and Fishing Zones Act extending the breadth of the territorial sea to twelve nautical miles. In the Arctic this had the practical effect of closing the northwest passage at its two narrowest points. The government further argued that the northwest passage, because of the ice cover, was not equivalent to an open-water international channel, and that as less than a dozen ships had ever transited it, there was no established right of international passage.

2. The Arctic Waters Pollution Prevention Act, to back up this assertion of sovereignty by establishing a hundred mile pollution control zone in Arctic waters north of 60° North latitude beyond the nearest Canadian land for purposes of extending Canadian anti-pollution and navigational safety jurisdiction, and requiring that all ships entering these waters conform to Canadian standards. Recognizing the legal novelty of this position, the government announced a reservation to its acceptance of the compulsory jurisdiction of the International Court of Justice (ICJ).

3. A further amendment to the Territorial Sea and Fishing Zones Act to establish Canadian jurisdiction for fisheries protection and anti-pollution purposes by drawing fisheries closing lines across the entrances of major bodies of water in special need of fisheries conservation protection. These bodies, the Gulf of Saint Lawrence, the Bay of Fundy, Dixon Entrance, Hecate Strait, and Queen Charlotte Sound, comprise 80,000 square miles of water beyond the twelve-mile territorial sea. The object was to establish effective controls over important fish breeding stocks while preserving the fisheries for Canadian fishermen. The government likewise reserved its position in the ICJ with regard to this legislation.

4. Amendments to the Canada Shipping Act within Canadian waters or waters under Canadian jurisdiction

(i.e. within the bodies of water enclosed within the fisheries closing lines) to enforce new and much stronger standards regarding ocean shipping to prevent pollution. This was as far as the government felt able to go in applying pollution controls in temperate waters.

The Arctic legislation did not go as far as the committee had proposed. Nevertheless, the device of establishing pollution-control zones was shrewdly chosen. It struck a responsive chord in the public mind both in the United States and in Canada and was keyed closely to concerns raised by the voyage of the Manhattan. Of special political importance, it produced a strong US protest, which led the leader of a Canadian opposition party to move that the bill be given unanimous consent, thereby protecting the government from further political criticism on a subject on which until that moment the opposition had been effectively attacking it. The measure of the government's success was that it achieved the rhetoric of confrontation with the United States without having to face an actual confrontation. For under the ice conditions which prevail year round in the northwest passage, there are no ships moving other than submarines and they travel—if they do—out of sight and therefore without publicly challenging the Canadian position.

At the time a far-reaching implication of the Arctic Waters Act was largely ignored—the application of the reservation to the jurisdiction of the International Court. For throughout the postwar period Canada had advocated the principle of increased use of the Court in resolving international disputes. The decision to enter reservations to the Court's jurisdiction was taken against strong opposition within the cabinet. However, few Canadians subsequently commented on the inconsistency between this unilateral action and the continuing Canadian emphasis on the importance of developing a new international law to prevent and control pollution hazards, apparently accepting the government's contention that the international legal community was still dominated by selfish states concerned first with preserving their shipping fleets. It is of course true that this act and the amendments to the Canada Shipping Act serve as an example and give leverage to Canada in future negotiations on marine pollution controls.[17] Recent British legislative changes, anticipating international acceptance of an Inter-Governmental Maritime Consultative Organization (IMCO) convention, to extend the government's power to destroy ships on the high seas which might threaten to pollute the British coastline, is a sign that there is some international movement in this direction.

To date ships have not sought approval for travelling within these zones. And with the decision of Humble Oil that sea transport across the Arctic is not commercially feasible at this time, there are no immediate prospects of shipping activity.[18] So there has not been, nor is there likely to be, an early test of the legislation. Foreign criticism there has been, but instead of raising doubts, these objections have reinforced the government's domestic support. Few questions have been raised in Canada as to whether the legislation was necessary or in keeping with the country's traditional views on international law and the Court. The government has successfully made the case that the setting of standards for Arctic sea transportation is itself desirable. Undoubtedly, the explanation for this considerable change in orientation is a widespread nationalist sentiment which approves this legislation as an assertion of Canadian independence against the United States and as an act designed indirectly to extend Canadian sovereignty over the uninhabited and unexploited but potentially rich Arctic frontier.

[17] One of the objectives pursued during Trudeau's visit to the USSR was to seek Soviet support, as the major Arctic power—and one taking an exclusionist view of the Arctic—for Canada's Arctic pollution-control legislation. With typical candour, the prime minister responded to the press questions on his return by admitting that ' so far, they've just stonewalled it '. (Office of PM, Transcript of interview with press reporters en route to Ottawa from Leningrad, 28 May 1971.)

[18] To enter Hudson Bay, ships must travel north of the 60° North latitude, and ships doing so should therefore be required to meet Canadian Arctic pollution-control standards. Churchill, Manitoba is an established port for shipping grain to Europe and during the short ice-free shipping season there are no unusual hazards on this route. Application of the standards to grain vessels might lead ship owners to withdraw from the route which is only usable for less than three months a year. Since port facilities in Canada for exporting grain are already overextended, since the route is established and used during a limited and controlled period of the year, and finally, since it is of major political importance in Canada that grain keep moving, it will be interesting to see whether the government exempts grain ships travelling to Churchill during the open season from the Arctic-pollution controls.

With the decision not to proceed with icebreaking tankers, public preoccupation with the whole question of Canadian sovereignty in the Arctic has died and the Trudeau government has emerged, tarnished perhaps in the eyes of the international legal community, but brightly burnished at home.

The government has continued to show interest in the development of the Arctic territories. As the prime minister remarked when announcing the decision to withdraw forces from Europe, ' we're beginning to realize now that we're not a one ocean country, not an Atlantic country, not even a two ocean country, an Atlantic and a Pacific, we're a three-ocean country. . . . And we're beginning to realize that in the Arctic, Canadian interests are very great.'[19] The government has invested directly in oil exploration, is increasing the Canadian military presence in the area, attempting to improve communications within this vast region, and generally trying to arouse public interest in this last frontier. Apart from the intrinsic benefits to be derived from this activity, it is deliberately intended to strengthen the basis for Canada's legal claims in the Arctic.

The problem of extracting north shore Alaska oil remains, however, and has become a new source of potential tension between Canada and the United States. The preferred choice of the owners of the oil rights has been to build a pipeline over Alaska to the Panhandle, to ship the oil by tanker down Canada's west coast to Puget Sound, and then to pipe it to centres of need in the United States. The opposition of American ecologists, concerned about the dangers of a giant pipeline crossing seismically active regions of Alaska, has caused delays in granting the permit needed to cross Alaska. This has given Canadians time to react, aroused as they are by the danger of mammoth pollution on the west coast, particularly in the strait of Juan de Fuca, lying between Vancouver Island and Washington State. But Canadian self-interest has also come into play. An alternative route for the oil would be along Canada's north shore to the Mackenzie River and up that valley to connect with pipelines running east and west from southern Alberta. Such

[19] Office of PM, transcript of a speech in Calgary, Alberta, 12 Apr. 1969.

a route would create considerable employment in the construction phase. It would also provide a sure means for transporting oil which may at any time be found in the Canadian Arctic, for if the Alaskan route is built, it may not be economical for many years to build a second pipeline down the Mackenzie. However, the all-US route is the more probable. If and when that decision is announced, Canadians will, in their frustration, loudly protest about the use of the west coast shipping channel and complain about the government's ineffectiveness, as they have previously done over US nuclear underground tests in the Aleutian Islands.

In anticipation of such an outcome, the government is pressing the United States to accept the international legal principle of responsibility for damage caused to neighbouring states. Canada wants an advance commitment from the United States to accept full financial liability for any damage caused in Canada by an accident on the high seas or in US territorial waters, and to count this as a cost of shipping the oil. Whatever the Americans finally agree to, if there is an accident as a result of this enterprise and the Canadian west coast is polluted, Canadian feelings against the United States would run very high. Acceptance of full liability by the Americans would help to limit the damage to bilateral relations, as would a decision to avoid the Strait of Juan de Fuca by transporting the oil directly to California for refining.

Fishing closing lines

The decision to enact fisheries closing lines legislation, thus closing large bodies of waters traditionally fished by foreigners, has had immediate and significant effects abroad. Among traditional fishermen of these Atlantic waters have been Norwegians, Danes, French, British, Spanish, Portuguese, and Americans. More recent arrivals are the Russians (both oceans) and the Japanese and Koreans in the Pacific. The Canadian government is in the process of negotiating agreements with all these countries to achieve an orderly withdrawal from these waters, the only exception being the Americans, with whom Canada has a reciprocal fishing agreement. The government's justification for these far-reaching measures is that modern deep-sea fishing techniques are so depleting fish stocks that they may threaten their survival. Not surprisingly, however, the aim in conserving fish stocks is to preserve important fisheries for Canadian fishermen who have continued to rely mainly on inshore fishing techniques. Even these measures have not satisfied Canadian fishing interests, who would like to see exclusive fishing zones established to the limit of the continental shelf, which in some places in the Atlantic extends out as far as 400 miles. But for the present the government has drawn the closing lines around definable bodies of water which can in some sense be claimed as recognizably Canadian.

While international protests have been directed as much against this legislation as against the Arctic pollution controls, interest and concern on the part of Canadians have been largely limited to inhabitants of the directly affected east and west coast areas—where feelings run very high and where the government's action is strongly supported, even though its effective application is considered to be too slow. For this is the test which counts for Canadian fishermen: not abstract principles of law, but when do the foreign fishermen move out? The broader and more nationalist approach of the bulk of Canadians can be seen from the following strongly-worded resolution adopted at the Liberal Policy Convention held in Ottawa in November 1970: 'We should declare sovereignty over the waters on the continental shelves and slopes below the Atlantic, Pacific and Arctic Oceans.' To this resolution, 607 Liberals strongly agreed, 289 more agreed, and 87 were not sure, while only 26 disagreed and 15 strongly disagreed. By contrast, a much milder and more limited resolution on the management and control of fishing zones actually attracted less support.

How to explain the widespread support for the Arctic legislation in contrast with the sectional interest in the fisheries legislation—both of which aroused strong international opposition? The Arctic legislation in popular terms was seen as a dramatic assertion of Canadian sovereignty against supposed US acquisitiveness. The fisheries legislation does not involve land in any respect. Much more important, the confrontation with the United States is blunted because, although the US government has protested the law, American fishermen are free to continue to fish in the waters concerned. This was a deliberate Canadian move to ensure that confrontation is kept within manageable limits. In any case, Canadian fishermen have few complaints against US fishermen because each has reciprocal fishing rights in the other's waters. Besides, over 80 per cent of Canadian fish is sold in the American market. The villains in this instance are all extra-continental, and they do not arouse the same instinctive emotional fears across the country.

Canada has not tried, as Mexico has, to exploit international law to protect itself from the United States. On the contrary, Canada has preferred to use politics and diplomacy to secure protection where necessary. The handling of the Arctic Pollution Control and Fisheries Closing Lines legislation has conformed with this tradition. Instead of seeking a legal compromise which could have gained international recognition, Canada decided on unilateral action in breach of established international law. This was done in full recognition of likely challenges by the United States and other countries, it being hoped by this means eventually to demonstrate the full extent of Canada's sovereignty and control in the Arctic and over other adjacent waters.

Continental integration

In this age, the economic benefits from integration have become more pronounced and regional groupings have proliferated. These developments have subjected Canadian relations with the United States to new strain, for Canada was founded as a denial of continentalism. The Canadian Pacific Railway, completed in 1885, was consciously intended to stimulate east–west links and to check the natural north–south tendencies. A national airline and the Canadian Broadcasting Corporation established in the 1930s had the same motive.

Such are the benefits of continental integration, however, that inevitably several arrangements linking the two countries have already been worked out where the benefits to be derived are mutual. The field of energy illustrates the technical and political problems of integration. The hydro grids of the province of Ontario and New York State are so interconnected that the failure in 1967 of a component the size of a thumb in a switching station in Ontario caused by chain reaction a twelve-hour blackout in New York City. Likewise, Canadian oil and gas finds a market in the United States, although not in the volume which Canadian producers desire, because it suits the United States to have alternative continental sources to make up some of its fuel deficiencies.

The National Energy Board of Canada must approve all export contracts. In November 1971 it refused three applications to export a total of 2·66 trillion cubic feet of natural gas (with a value of approximately $1 billion) on the ground that Canadian reserves were inadequate. This judgement has been challenged by the industry, and will undoubtedly be regretted by the US authorities who are desperately looking for ' clean ' sources of fuel. However, the United States has itself embargoed uranium imports since 1962 when United States domestic production reached sufficiency. This has caused considerable distress in Canada because, in response to US wartime and postwar military requirements, production had grown rapidly to a point where in 1959 it was a leading export, with a value at the time of over $300 million. Since Canada restricts sales to other countries to peaceful uses, exports are very limited and the domestic market is equally small. The industry has been in distress for a decade.

Economic logic suggests there should be a continental energy policy, particularly since the industry is largely American owned and US political and business leaders are pressing hard for acceptance by Canada of such an approach. There are, of course, attractions. For example, Canada could bargain for renewed access to the US uranium market. But, apart from the complexity of such negotiations, Canadians are reluctant even to accept the principle. In its crudest terms, this fear is expressed by a slogan now current in some circles in Canada: ' continentalism is treason '. In more sophisticated terms, this attitude has been documented by an eminent and highly concerned Canadian historian, surveying the Canadian nation's first 100 years, who concluded that by 1967:

Continentalism had divorced Canadians from their history, crippled their creative capacity and left them without the power to fashion a new future for themselves. Even the will to defend their independence and protect their national identity had become weakened; they scarcely seemed to be aware of the danger in which they stood.[20]

There are a few very successful examples—in Canadian eyes at any rate—of limited co-operative arrangements. The Canada–United States Automotive Agreement of 1965 provides for free trade in automobiles and spare parts. Its effect has been dramatic. Between 1963 and 1966 Canadian exports to the United States of motor vehicles and parts increased from $37 million to $841 million.[21] This has led some Canadians to look to free trade for salvation. But conditions in the industry are unique: all the major Canadian producers of completed automobiles (as distinct from spare parts and components) are entirely American-owned, so that continental-wide rationalization—which has been accomplished—is achieved within each corporation. Secondly, the agreement provides certain guarantees of production being maintained in Canada, so that the forces of the market are not fully free to operate. The general conclusion is that this scheme would not work in other industries, and even in this instance there is growing resistance within the US government to its continuance in its present form.

The Defence Production Sharing Agreement is another unique North American co-operative industrial programme. In 1959, following the collapse of Canada's efforts to build independently a supersonic jet fighter, the Arrow, and taking account of the integrated air-defence arrangements that had just been established for the continent, a bilateral defence production sharing arrangement was worked out. The United States agreed to waive customs duties and the application of the Buy America Act to Canada, giving Canadian manufacturers an equal chance to bid against US domestic producers for military contracts. The two governments subsequently in 1963 agreed to try to maintain over the long term their military procurement in the other country in rough balance.

In many respects the agreement has been a very great success. Initially the balance was heavily in the American favour, reflecting the situation which prevailed before the agreement was

[20] D. G. Creighton, *Canada's First Century* (1970), p. 355.
[21] *Canada Year Book, 1965, 1968.*

signed: in 1960 Canada exported $112·7 million to the United
States while importing $196·3 million.[22] But by 1962 this arms
trade was in balance. For the last several years—with demand
stimulated by the Vietnam war—the balance has been heavily
in Canada's favour, although this situation is probably changing. The Canadian electronics and aircraft industries have until
recently found an important market through this agreement,
the more significant for Canada because both are areas of
advanced technology. In comparison with production-sharing
agreements among NATO allies in Europe, the achievement
has been remarkable. Total defence trade from 1959 to 1970 has
reached a cumulative total of almost $5 billion.

In spite of its success and the jobs which flow from it (15,000
directly and over 100,000 indirectly),[23] the agreement is under
some attack in Canada from the left. Opposition to the Vietnam
war is the main impulse. Critics would like to see Canada follow
Sweden's example and stop all arms sales to the United States,
or at least of those arms being sent to Vietnam. This line of
criticism has, however, been espoused by only one minor party
(the New Democratic Party). For, unlike Sweden, which gave
up arms sales of only $1 million and which can afford the
gesture because it is far removed from the United States,
Canada must weigh more carefully the effect of such a step on
its relations with the United States, for the economic consequences for Canada which would obviously be drastic. Moreover, Canadians are certainly more understanding of the US
dilemma in Vietnam than are the Swedes.

Apart from the political liabilities of the agreement, which
are probably linked mainly to the Vietnam war, it has had
economic consequences not fully anticipated when it was made.
At that time Canada was producing a variety of finished arms,
and it was expected this would continue. In practice, Canada's
exports in the arms goods industry have been largely made up of
components with a high technological content for assembly in
the United States, which means that the agreement has
advanced the integration of the two economies. This development has produced caution and increased hesitation about

[22] *External Affairs*, May 1961, p. 175.
[23] Parl., H. of C. SCEAND, *11th Report*, 1970, p. 19.

advancing towards free trade with the Americans. The automotive agreement has been scrutinized too and one trend noted with concern: continental integration of the industry has in practical terms meant that fewer key planning decisions are made in Canada and the net charge for management advice supplied by the United States to the Canadian components of the industry has increased. There is also some concern about diminished autonomy in the Canadian section of the international auto workers' union.

Thus even the success stories have their warnings and have contributed to Canadian anxieties about plunging headlong into the embrace of continentalism. Since the United States has shown a similar reticence,[24] Canadian policy in this field will continue to be cautious, hesitant, very pragmatic, with each proposal being considered more or less in isolation.

Approach to bilateral relations

The ad hoc approach has been characteristic of the whole range of policies for dealing with the United States. The only effort to develop an integrated approach was made in 1965. A former Canadian and a former American ambassador in each country's capital, A. D. P. Heeney and L. T. Merchant, were asked by Prime Minister Pearson, and President Johnson to prepare a report on how the two countries should consult and treat each other. However, their report was attacked by Diefenbaker as taking too compliant an approach to the Americans and it appears never to have been seriously considered.

The multiplicity and range of Canadian links with the United States have led to the development of a variety of functional instruments for resolving differences. These, of course, go beyond the normal official diplomatic contacts, which are vast in number. In 1968 the Department of External Affairs calculated that there were 12,900 official Canadian visits to Washington,[25]

[24] In a report of 13 Sept. 1971, the president's Commission on International Trade and Investment Policy cautioned ' that any further sectoral approaches to US-Canadian free trade be subjected to the closest possible scrutiny before commitments are undertaken . . . [and] that the overall US-Canadian relationship—political as well as economic—would be better served by a world-wide rather than a bilateral reduction of trade barriers '.

[25] SCEAND, *Mins. of Proc. & Evidence*, 3 Nov. 1969, p. 3: 64.

and this takes no account of the meetings at international conferences and other continuous correspondence and telephone communications between the related departments of government. What becomes evident is the degree to which relations with the United States impinge on domestic Canadian policy-making.

In an effort to de-politicize some of these relationships and to minimize Canada's disadvantages which result from its relatively smaller size, recourse has been had to quasi-autonomous institutions, mostly advisory, others with limited executive powers, to handle specific bilateral functions. The first of these was the International Boundary Commission established as early as 1908. The International Joint Commission is another. Established in 1911, this joint body has dealt recently with boundary waters pollution, and on its recommendation agreement was reached in June 1971 for a co-operative programme to clean up pollution in the Great Lakes. The meeting which concluded the agreement was of particular interest because it included representation from the provinces of Ontario and Quebec and border states in the United States.

The principle governing Canadian dealings with the United States—that every issue should be treated separately—has remained unchallenged over the years. There are advocates of the contrary view who hold that Canada should try to exploit areas of advantage, such as the US need for natural gas, to gain benefits in areas where Canada's bargaining position is weaker. The effect of such an approach would, however, be to raise the level of negotiations from the technical to the political, and ultimately to raise questions in the minds of the US president and his cabinet about the whole direction of relations with Canada. Moreover, in such broad negotiations, the balance of advantage would be with the United States as the stronger party. These arguments were persuasive to the House Committee on External Affairs and National Defence which recommended in its 11th report of June 1970: ' In fields involving continuing co-operation with the United States, . . . consideration should be given to the use of bilateral bodies where representatives of the two countries meet as equals ' (p. 66). There is every reason to expect these principles to continue to guide Canadian governments in their future negotiations with the United States. Nevertheless, Canada could derive advantage from developing an integrated strategy for dealing with the United States in order to ensure that as the weaker partner, Canadian interests were promoted as effectively as possible.

The US import surcharge

Because of Canada's high proportion of foreign trade and concentration on the American market, President Nixon's drastic programme of 15 August 1971 for attacking the US foreign-exchange deficit would have had an especially severe effect on Canada's economy. Even though three-quarters of Canadian exports to the United States were exempted from the 10 per cent surcharge, 3 per cent of the entire GNP was directly affected by it. This meant that Canada was more severely affected than any other state. Rough calculations suggested that 40,000–100,000 workers would lose their jobs if the surcharge remained in effect for a year, which would have meant up to 1 per cent increase in the already high level of unemployment.

Because of the intimate economic links between the two countries, the United States twice in the last decade agreed, following urgent representations, to exempt Canada from the application of earlier programmes intended to cope with its foreign-exchange problems: the Interest Equalization Tax of 1963 and the mandatory regulations regarding direct capital investment of 1968. In both instances the American authorities were persuaded that Canada, then running a sizeable trade deficit with the United States, was more helpful if its economy remained healthy. It was not surprising, therefore, that the first move of the Canadian government after President Nixon's speech, was again to seek some exemption, pointing to the exceptional severity of the impact on Canada, to the absence of obstacles in the way of American imports, and to the fact that Canada, with a floating exchange rate, had already allowed market forces to determine an appropriate rate of exchange. But the appeal was rejected. Although no reasons were given, the US authorities stressed in private that Canada's current trade surplus with the United States, stimulated by earlier American agreements to open their market freely to Canadian automobile and defence goods sales, represented the largest single recent shift in their balance-of-payments picture. The implication was conveyed that to overcome the US deficit, it would be necessary to force Canada again into a deficit position. And since the United States needs Canadian raw materials, this means that all the cuts would have to be in exports of manufactured goods. In Canada some importance is also attached to the dominant position of the Secretary of the Treasury, Governor Connally of Texas, who—unlike his Eastern seaboard predecessors—does not have a special feeling for the Canadian–American relationship.

The rejection of the plea for exemption left the Canadian government uncertain where to turn next. On television on 23 September the prime minister's tone conveyed the government's doubts:

> ... we're trying to analyze whether the United States have made a fundamental change. . . . I don't think that the United States is deliberately trying to beggar its neighbours and make this into a permanent policy. . . . If . . . they just want us to be sellers of natural resources to them and buyers of their manufactured products . . . we will have to reassess fundamentally our relation with them, trading, political and otherwise . . . they will have to realize that Canadians are also a proud nation and that if they are really trying to rearrange the North American Continent so that we are just a supplier of natural resources and that we won't be able to find jobs for our growing labour force and we won't be able to have an advanced technological society that we can manage ourselves, that is a very, very serious hypothesis. . . . I would certainly want to make sure that President Nixon is aware of the dilemma he is creating for Canada in terms of our future orientation in this North American Continent.[26]

Several months later, on 6 December 1971, Trudeau undertook a brief trip to Washington to ensure that President Nixon was indeed made personally aware of the Canadian position, and

> to seek reassurance from the President . . . that it is neither the intention nor the desire of the United States that the economy of Canada become so dependent on the United States in terms of a

[26] Office of PM, transcript.

deficit trading pattern that Canadians will inevitably lose independence of economic decision.

The prime minister described the meeting as a ' breakthrough ' and on his return told the Commons that the president had assured him ' it was in the interests of the United States to have a Canadian neighbour which was independent both politically and economically '. Nixon had been ' sensitive to the suggestion that his 15 August policies could be interpreted as evidence that the United States was unable to accept a Canada with a strong trading and current account position vis-à-vis the United States . . . but [the president] stated to me forcefully that [this interpretation] was incorrect'.[27] Two weeks later, on 19 December, at the meeting of the Group of Ten in Washington, it was agreed that the dollar would be devalued by 7·9 per cent in terms of gold and the US 10 per cent import charge would be lifted immediately. It was further agreed that the Canadian dollar would continue to float, as it has since June 1970, and the Canadian authorities reiterated that they would not intervene in the market to hold down the value of the dollar.

The Nixon measures made the Canadian government sharply aware of the extent of Canadian vulnerability to economic and fiscal measures taken by Washington for legitimate internal reasons. The shock pushed the government into undertaking a fundamental review of the whole Canadian relationship with the United States. The options explored—in the greatest detail —run from seeking a free trade area with the United States (which would be unacceptable politically), through maintaining the present ' ad hoc ' approach, to making a conscious and broad effort, using every aspect of public policy, to diminish Canada's dependence on the United States. Despite the lifting of the surcharge, programmes for reducing this dependency are almost inevitable, and are likely to be announced before the government calls an election, i.e. sometime before November 1972. Canadian policy toward the United States will never again be as trusting as it has been in the past.

[27] H. of C. Deb., 7 Dec. 1971, p. 10205.

6

EUROPE: CANADA'S LAST CHANCE?

EUROPEAN nations are understandably preoccupied with the questions posed and the opportunities offered by the enlargement of the EEC. They are responding in the main with confidence to the drift towards continentalism because integration is seen as a way of balancing off more powerful neighbours and so of reducing the fear that smaller nations naturally feel of external domination. Not so for Canada, where the movement towards continentalism—one of the great movements of the second half of the twentieth century—poses very serious problems, since Canada alone shares virtually the entire North American continent with the United States.

Canada's relations with the United States are dominated by psychological insecurity. By contrast, the nations of Europe have long histories of distinct cultural identities even where independence is actually only an achievement of this century. This sense of identity has been built up over centuries of conflict with neighbouring but culturally distinct and historically conscious peoples. Canada represented in many respects until the last generation a deliberate denial of this tradition and process. The main requirements for Canadian citizenship were five years' residence and an oath of allegiance to respect the laws of the country. Canada rejected the American concept of the melting pot and made no strong effort to forge a common loyalty and identity in its immigrants. The result in Canada was a kind of cultural patchwork quilt of peoples linked by tolerance for each other and respect for common institutions. Politically until a generation ago the main external preoccupation was reshaping ties with Britain, the mother country, and an attempt to remain isolated from the conflicts and rivalries which were seen as the careless sport of Europeans.

In North America, once the boundaries had been agreed

upon, a process largely completed by 1867, Canadians and Americans could proceed to develop their separate parts of the continent virtually in isolation one from the other.

In all this process the French Canadians represented and continue to represent an anomaly, a people culturally and historically distinct, consciously struggling to preserve their identity and even their existence. But this struggle was essentially defensive, fought, as in Slovakia, at the parish level and having few manifestations at the broader political levels. Although at first sight the French Canadians and the Mexicans appear to share common problems, the Mexicans are more numerous, they have their own country which they have defended by their own efforts against attack from the United States and intervention from Europe and, most important, they are part of the Latin American cultural world and so do not fear assimilation by the English-language culture of North America.

The great movement throughout the world towards integration has placed new values and benefits on such historic attitudes. An assurance of cultural identity is now a necessary psychological support to giving up sovereignty within a larger impersonal entity. Europeans have the further advantage that their continent is divided between several larger and not so large nations, so that in combination they balance each other off rather than acquire a new instrument for establishing hegemony. Canada has neither of these advantages. Only the French Canadians are culturally distinct from Americans; English-speaking Canadians really are not, however much they would like to be. And unavoidably any normal arrangements for continental integration place the Americans in a position of dominance.

British entry into the EEC

It may come as a shock to British readers to find separate chapters devoted to Canadian relations with France and the United States, while the British connection is dealt with rather summarily in a chapter on Europe. This treatment has been consciously selected to reflect the actual situation; historical links have only been noted where these are necessary for better understanding of present policies or conditions. Thus, in spite of past imperial and present Commonwealth ties with Britain, these are now seen mainly in policy terms as part of a larger link with the new Europe, with which Britain by its own decision is merging. Unlike France and the United States, which in different ways have become threats to Canada's survival, Britain represents no challenge to any vital Canadian interest. While Britain's entry into the Common Market will cause some adjustment in trade, Canadians have already accommodated to the inevitability of this development and now view it as being quite natural.

The main aim of Canadian foreign policy during the inter-war period was the development of practical independence from Britain within what became known as the Commonwealth. This had to be done gradually, partly because an important minority of Canadian opinion retained a deep sense of loyalty to Britain and partly because Canada remained dependent on the United Kingdom for markets and for capital. But while Canadians now have emotional problems in dealing with the United States, they used, until very recently, to have similar hang-ups towards the British and French. For English-speaking and French-speaking Canadians, particularly of the older generation, the emotional consequences of past colonial relationships with Britain and with France have produced some of the unfortunate effects of the parent-child syndrome. The relationship for Quebeckers has been complicated by France's long scorn and neglect and by their present need for cultural contact and support from France. Although the emotional tensions caused by these historical and cultural associations should not be exaggerated, they explain in some degree the lack of enthusiasm in Canada for turning to the old world to redress the balance of the new, as the French journalist Claude Julien has suggested: ' Seule l'Europe peut éviter l'absorption économique du Canada par les Etats-Unis, absorption qui réduirait Ottawa à ne plus être, sur le plan politique, qu'un pâle reflet de Washington '.[1]

The rapid world movement towards integration is facing Canadians with cruel choices. Canada found balance in the

[1] *Le Canada, dernière chance de l'Europe* (Paris, 1965), p. 13.

postwar world economically by espousing international efforts to achieve freer trade and politically through active participation in multilateral organizations such as NATO and the UN. This approach was nationally acceptable, in that it made unnecessary a choice among Canada's closest associates—the United States, Britain, and France. But it failed to prevent the concentration of Canadian trade with the United States or the growth of US investment in Canada. Now even the rationale for this policy is being undermined by events in Europe. Manifestly NATO, as a symbol of Atlantic unity and as a forum for its elaboration, is no longer the moving force there, although the Canadian government continues to express a desire to participate in any European Security Conference which may be held. Instead the momentum rests with the EEC, which is both widening its membership and expanding its area of responsibility.

So long as General de Gaulle kept Britain out of Europe, Canadians could ignore this development, and most did so. For Canada's trade with the United Kingdom alone remains—in spite of the steady decline in its relative importance—larger than its trade with the six Common Market countries combined. Understandably, but mistakenly, the response of the Diefenbaker government, in power at the time of Britain's first unsuccessful bid for entry, was to bewail the consequences for Canada. This message was so vigorously expounded, particularly by the then high commissioner in London, that some British regarded it as intervention in the internal debate in the United Kingdom. In the event, de Gaulle's abrupt dismissal of the British application removed the problem from front stage for Canadians for the decade. In 1971 it could no longer be ignored. However, the lesson had been learned, and the present Canadian government has been ultra-cautious in commenting for fear that a chance remark might be taken up in the British debate.

Britain's share of Canadian trade has fallen steadily since World War II. Although Diefenbaker came to power in 1957 with the declared intention of restoring British trade to its prewar level of relative importance, Britain's share of the Canadian market actually fell during his years in office as is shown in the first table on p. 90.

Canada's Trade with the United Kingdom

Year	%	Exports to Britain Value ($ millions)	%	Imports from Britain Value ($ millions)
1939	34·2	328·1	15·1	114·0
1947	27·1	746·1	7·2	184·2
1952	17·4	744·5	9·0	351·5
1957	15·1	720·9	9·3	507·3
1962	14·7	909·0	9·0	563·1
1967	10·5	1,169·1	6·1	673·1
1970	8·8	1,480·0	5·3	738·0
1971	7·7	1,361·0	5·3	832·0

Sources: *Canada Year Book, 1950*, pp. 907–8; *1968*, p. 959; *Foreign Trade*, 10 Apr. 1971, p. 24; *Canada Commerce*, Apr. 1972, p. 5.

The principal beneficiary has been the United States, whose imports from Canada have grown remarkably, as is shown below:

Canada's Trade with the United States

Year	%	Exports to Value ($ millions)	%	Imports from Value ($ millions)
1939	31·2	380·4	66·1	496·9
1947	37·4	1,030·1	76·8	1,951·6
1952	53·8	2,302·7	73·7	2,887·6
1957	59·4	2,846·6	71·0	3,887·4
1962	58·4	3,608·4	68·7	4,299·5
1967	63·7	7,073·4	72·4	8,016·3
1970	65·0	10,641·1	71·7	9,905·1
1971	67·8	12,006·0	70·2	10,949·0

Sources: as for table above.

In spite of the now relatively small proportion of Canadian exports going to Britain, their total value amounted to $1·5 billion in 1970 and the government is necessarily concerned about the effect on them of British entry into the EEC. Moreover, for a few Canadian industries the British market accounts for 90 per cent of total foreign sales. British entry is doubly damaging because Canada stands both to lose the preferential or free access it has enjoyed to date in the British market and to face reverse preferences which will cover imports from Common Market partners and other states having associate status with the EEC. It has been calculated that about 43 per cent of Canadian exports (mainly raw materials) will retain free entry into Britain because they already have free entry to the EEC, while another 11 per cent (mainly wood products) have been the subject of special arrangements obtained in the entry negotiations which will protect the Canadian position. This leaves some 45 per cent of exports, now amounting to about $670 million, which will face more difficult access conditions.[2] Of the most important commodities in this category, aluminium exports had already begun to decline owing to increased domestic production in the United Kingdom, and wheat could have been expected to suffer in any case from the combination of new milling techniques and the recently introduced British variable levy.

Quite evidently British entry is going to cause a dislocation in existing trade and probably the proportion of Canada's exports to the United Kingdom will continue to decline. Nevertheless Canada among the Commonwealth countries has the lowest proportion of its trade with Britain, so that the adjustment should be less difficult than for Britain's other Commonwealth partners. Of course, the long-term hope is that entry into the Common Market will stimulate growth in the sluggish British economy and that traditional contacts with British firms will lead to expanded Canadian sales throughout the EEC. It was notable that when the British prime minister visited Ottawa on 17 December 1971, en route for talks with Nixon in Bermuda, it was reported that discussions on British entry were harmonious.

Canada's trade performance with Common Market countries has not paralleled rates of growth within the EEC, although exports to the latter have expanded at a more rapid pace than exports to Britain. Thus, from 1965 to 1970 exports to the Common Market almost doubled from $625 million to $1·2 billion, while exports to Britain only increased by 25 per cent, from $1·2 billion to $1·5 billion. The EEC also takes a larger volume of manufactured goods ($160 million compared to $107 million to Britain), so important in the creation of employment. But in general the rate of growth of Canadian exports to

[2] Geoffrey Elliot, ' Enlargement of the EEC ', *Foreign Trade* (Ottawa), Sept. 1971, p. 4.

the EEC countries actually declined after the Common Market came into existence, and ' Canadian exports to the EEC grew at a slower rate than both world exports to the EEC and Canadian exports to the rest of the world '.[3] While the economic development of the Common Market in the last decade has brought absolute increases in trade with Canada, their relative importance has declined slightly (see table below) as Canadian trade with the United States and Japan has shot ahead.

Canada's Trade with the EEC

	Exports to EEC		Imports from EEC	
		Value		*Value*
Year	%	*($ millions)*	%	*($ millions)*
1961	8·1	465·6	5·5	318·2
1962	7·4	454·9	5·3	335·0
1963	7·0	474·6	5·2	341·6
1964	6·9	555·1	5·4	405·7
1965	7·3	625·8	6·0	514·2
1966	6·3	636·7	5·6	550·6
1967	6·1	677·2	5·6	626·6
1968	5·7	748·4	5·4	661·6
1969	5·8	837·0	5·6	789·2
1970	7·1	1,204·4	5·8	804·7
1971	6·2	1,101·0	6·0	935·0

Sources: *Canada Year Book: 1965*, pp. 916–17; *1968*, pp. 959, 964; *Foreign Trade*, 10 Apr. 1971, p. 24; *Canada Commerce*, Apr. 1972, p. 4.

Within these gross figures, the composition of Canadian exports to the EEC has shown considerable variation, with industrial raw materials and semi-processed goods increasing significantly, sales of manufactures holding steady, and agricultural exports declining. From 1955 to 1967 the value of total Canadian agricultural exports to the EEC rose slightly from US$165 million to US$192 million, but the dollar value of wheat sales actually remained steady at about $110 million. This disappointing Canadian performance is widely blamed on the Common Agricultural Policy (CAP) of the EEC; yet grain sales to the EFTA countries, which have no common import and production policies, have done no better, a fact that has been largely ignored in Canada. Developments beyond

[3] Bank of Montreal, *Business Review*, 30 June 1971.

Canada's control account for some of this relative decline in wheat sales in Europe: the discovery of new milling techniques which permit increased use of softer wheats grown in Europe and the introduction of improved agricultural practices and of support systems which have stimulated grain production in Europe. But Canadian deficiencies are also partly to blame: failure to introduce until August 1971 the protein scale for grading wheat, now the accepted international standard, and neglect of the competitive Western European market for some years after the large bulk sales negotiated with the USSR and China.

The EEC is normally pictured in Canada as being a restrictionist, high-tariff trading bloc, whereas its common external tariff for non-agricultural products is actually on the average lower than that of other major trading countries, including the United States and Canada. Admittedly, access is made more difficult by obstructive non-tariff barriers, yet this is also true to a certain degree elsewhere. However, it is the CAP which has given the Common Market its poor reputation in Canada, particularly since subsidized EEC grains cut out Canadian sales in some traditional markets.

Even all of this critical sentiment has been slow to awaken the Canadian government and the people to the importance, political and economic, of the growth of the European Community. The dual accreditation of the Canadian ambassador in Brussels to the EEC occurred in 1960, and by September 1971 only five of the seventeen other Canadian diplomatic officers in Brussels were responsible for relations with the EEC. There are still no plans for a separate head-of-state mission to the EEC, and it was not until 1970 that a Canadian cabinet minister visited EEC headquarters.

Only the imminence of British entry into the Common Market has finally begun to arouse widespread Canadian interest in the organization. The secretary of state for external affairs and the minister of industry, trade and commerce separately visited the EEC headquarters in Brussels in the autumn of 1970 and both were impressed by what they learned. Yet the government's response to the rapid evolution of the EEC, as set out in *Foreign Policy for Canadians*, displays much bureaucratic caution.

It is not inconceivable, that, within a relatively short period, the whole of Western Europe could become a single trading market as a result of the expanded membership or association arrangements built around the Community. As a matter of some urgency therefore, careful consideration should be given to the development of appropriate consultative arrangements which will take account of mutual Canada–EEC interests.[4]

But the establishment of ' appropriate consultative arrangements ' is no simple task. For the EEC is essentially the drawing together of states within a continent. The only exceptions have been for newly independent nations with past colonial connections, and Canada's colonial past is too remote to qualify.

The traditional Canadian response for coping with this kind of problem has been to advocate general free trade. Yet this offers no solution in a situation such as that which emerged in the Kennedy Round negotiations, when the essentials of all agreements were negotiated between the EEC and the United States, and Canada and other countries were limited to kibitzing from the sidelines. Special economic arrangements with the Common Market would be of interest to Canada, but how would this affect the advantageous position Canada now has in the US market? Indeed, is Canada not to some degree locked by geography into North America? On the European side there would obviously be an insistence on excluding agriculture for any special arrangements, since free entry of Canadian grains would probably undermine the CAP—Canada in this respect being the Japan of grain production.

Apart from discretely pressing the United Kingdom during the negotiations with the EEC to hold out for terms which would cause the least dislocation to Canadian exports, the Canadian government has taken none of the broader decisions which flow from the enlargement of the Community. Trade minister Pepin's visit to West Germany in April 1971 accompanied by a large group of Canadian businessmen demonstrated the government's interest in increasing trade with some European countries. But by and large the near-miraculous performance of Canadian exports during the last decade has made less urgent the search for a more aggressive and imaginative

[4] *FPC: Europe,* p. 21.

approach to trading with the Common Market. Such has been the growth in Canada's exports that from a position a decade earlier when the current-account[5] deficit amounted to $1,200 million, by 1970 Canada had a favourable balance of $1,297 million, by far the most spectacular advance being made in the single year 1970, the first year since 1952 that an actual surplus was recorded. In the same decade 1960–70 the surplus on merchandise trade jumped from $313 million in 1960 to $3,002 million,[6] the latter figure almost four times the previous year's total. This phenomenal growth in exports has continued in spite of the decision in May 1970 to allow the Canadian dollar to float freely, as a result of which it has risen from 92·5 cents to the US dollar to about 98 cents. Even this premium of more than 5 per cent has scarcely been reflected in reduced exports, although the important paper industry has suffered, and the foreign exchange reserves rose to US$4,845 million early in 1971.[7] However, the improvement in the export of Canadian manufacturers owes much to the free access to the United States' automobile and defence goods markets. And the potential impact of the economic measures announced by President Nixon in August 1971 demonstrated how vulnerable is the Canadian economy to action by the United States. This gives added importance to a policy of intensifying Canadian economic links with the countries of Europe.

Relations with Europe

The Trudeau government has not as yet developed an overall view of what Canada's relations with Europe should be. The booklet in *Foreign Policy for Canadians* concerning relations with Europe was a highly competent survey of the main developments on that continent, with a sound analysis of their implications for Canada and a number of useful suggestions for expanding contacts with European countries and institutions in ways which might lessen the United States' overwhelming influence

---

[5] The current-account balance or deficit includes 'invisibles', such as interest and dividends on investments, shipping charges and travel expenditures, as well as the merchandise trade balance or deficit figures.

[6] Dom. Bureau Statist., *The Canadian Balance of International Payments* (1967), p. 10; *Quarterly Estimates of Canadian Balance of Payments*, June 1971, pp. 20–1.

[7] *Quarterly Estimates of Canadian Balance of Payments*, June 1971, pp. 30–1.

on Canada. But it read more like a newspaper editorial than a statement of government policy, full of exhortations where there should be assertions. And the policy paper *Europe* candidly acknowledged that, ' aware of fundamental changes both in Europe and Canada, the Government is determining its objectives and priorities in terms of these realities ' (p. 30). This process has still not been completed.

In objective terms the countries of Western Europe, including Britain, jointly represent the one area of the world with which Canada has a range and breadth of relationships which could to some degree serve to offset the weight of the United States. Apart from trading relations, which have already been detailed, Europe has become in the last decade a substantial source of equity investment and, more recently, of medium-term financing, all of which reduces Canadian dependency on US sources of finance. Europe has also been the primary source of immigrants. According to the 1961 census, 96 per cent of all Canadians had European forebears and 14 per cent of the population had actually been born in Europe. This movement has left a vast network of continuing personal relationships, which is reflected in tourist travel between the two continents. In fact, almost 80 per cent of all Canadian tourist dollars spent abroad (outside of the United States) are spent in continental Europe and the United Kingdom, and Canadians take over 400,000 trips to that area in an average year.[8] Although the reverse flow is smaller, the bulk of non-American visitors to Canada come from Europe.

This brief catalogue of Canada's contacts with Europe can be rivalled by no other part of the world. Even though Canada–Japan trade and investment contacts are growing rapidly, they do not compare with the combined European figures, and Japan has none of the other cultural or personal links which give so much depth to the Canadian–European connection. Nor has there been a shared history, nor the intimate involvement in war and in the subsequent fight for peace which can weld such enduring links. All of which means that Europe alone can counterbalance the influence of the United States.

This concept of counterweight has to be carefully assessed. It

[8] *Canada Year Book, 1968*, p. 1003. Figures are for 1966.

is not a matter of seeking to end the primacy of the United States in Canada's external relations; that would be impossible. The object is to reduce Canada's dependence on the United States to a point—which will vary over time—sufficient to overcome the sense of psychological subordination. It is not suggested that Europe replace the United States as Canada's principal source of trade and investments; only that an effort be made to increase the proportion of Canada's exports to Europe, which with Britain in the Common Market, will now amount to more than 15 per cent of the present total. Given the poor Canadian performance in Europe in the last decade, a determined effort should produce results which might be enough to have psychological significance. To do this successfully, however, would require more than a trade-promotion programme. The government would have to mount a co-ordinated and concerted effort to focus Candian attention on Europe.

This is not likely to happen for the present. Other than for touring and visiting one's forebears, Europe is not in vogue among Canada's intellectuals as a focus for the nation's external activity. Europe is widely regarded in these quarters as being either selfish and sated, or old hat and insufficiently challenging; besides, it offers no outlet for humanitarian activity. Making a case for increased assistance to the third world, Professor Thomas Hockin argued for reduced involvement in Europe—which in 1968 and 1969 meant withdrawing troops—and urged greater ' voluntarism ', i.e. altruism, in Canadian policy.

To maintain Europe as a major focus of Canadian foreign policy is as untenable for Canada now as a neutralist or isolationist policy would be. Voluntarism and anti-militarism do not lead to neutralism about Europe and isolationism outside of Europe. They lead now to arenas outside Europe where Canadians could see if their voluntarism can do some good instead of having it continually frustrated in the European arena.[9]

It is difficult to judge how long this bias against Europe will prevail. The issue in debate in Canada in 1969 was

[9] L. Hertzman & others, *Alliances and Illusions* (1969), p. 127.

pre-eminently the question of forces in Europe. Critics like Hockin who favoured force withdrawal tended to argue in terms of alternative world needs and opportunity costs, while most defenders based their case on the military necessity of a Canadian force of 10,000 men—and on the proposition that Europe was Canada's first line of defence. In the ensuing debate the larger question of the importance of Europe to Canada and of the relevance of Canadian forces in Europe to this relationship was never adequately discussed. And once the decision was taken to reduce these forces by 5,000 men, the whole question of Canada and Europe strangely ceased to arouse public interest.

Canadians are, in fact, extraordinarily ignorant about what is happening in the new Europe. Institutes for the study of Africa, Asia, the Commonwealth, and Latin America proliferate, but there is only one important centre [10] in Canada for the study of the EEC, and since it is working in French its studies are scarcely known to the majority of English-speaking Canadians.

Canada and the new Europe

European integration is transforming world relationships. Strategically, with the inevitable reduction of US forces in Europe, the Continental members of NATO, now mainly linked in large part also through the EEC, will draw closer together as they rely increasingly on their own efforts. Politically, Europe is moving towards a new kind of federal system, by a pragmatic process which deliberately obscures this objective in order to hasten its achievement. Economically, the enlarged EEC will be responsible for 40 per cent of the world's trade and its imports are substantially larger than those of the United States. In view of these really fantastic developments of little more than a decade, the disregard of academics and until recently of policy-makers is a remarkable comment on Canadian myopia.

Fortunately, there are signs that official policy is now changing. In addition to the visits by Sharp and Pepin to the EEC headquarters, both ministers have visited major European

[10] Le Centre d'Etudes et de Documentation Européennes in Montreal.

countries in 1970 and again in 1971.[11] Their efforts have in turn begin to evoke a response on the part of Europeans who, preoccupied with their own internal developments, have tended in the past to regard Canada as being irrevocably tied economically to the United States. President Nixon's economic measures have stimulated on both sides of the Atlantic Ocean an awareness of mutual interest; Canadian concerns in respect of trade, although not of monetary policy, closely parallel those of Europe. The visit to Ottawa of Franco Malfatti, then president of the EEC Commission, was an important indication of the response which these Canadians' efforts have finally begun to evoke in Europe. Just as important, Sharp's statement on the occasion of that visit was by far the most positive affirmation of Canadian interest in the new Europe.

Les récentes mesures américaines . . . soulignent aussi . . . l'importance fondamentale que prennent à nos yeux nos relations commerciales et autres avec l'Europe et particulièrement avec la Communauté. Votre visite au Canada constitue un nouveau pas vers un coopération plus étroite entre le gouvernement canadien et la Commission économique européenne. Nous nous proposons de notre côté de renforcer et d'accroître nos mécanismes de consultations avec votre groupe. Votre présence aujourd'hui est pour nous la preuve que la Commission entend travailler dans le même sens.[12]

The measure of the Canadian problem can be seen from the public treatment of Malfatti's visit. The press paid little attention to his presence in Canada and there was no public discussion of what opportunities are open to Canada for entering into regular and more formal contact with the EEC of the kind implied by Sharp. For reasons discussed earlier, associate status of any kind is impossible. Canada could opt for regular consultations (known colloquially as the Samuels–Dahrendorf formula), as the United States has done. But this precedent is unsuited to Canadian needs because the contacts are at the under-secretary level (American under-secretaries having

---

[11] The leader of the opposition, Robert Stanfield, scooped the government with a month's visit to Europe during the summer of 1970. He spent two days at the Commission headquarters and on his return to Canada spoke and wrote of the need for Canada to pay increased attention to the EEC.

[12] 15 Sept. 1971. Text provided by Dept. of External Affairs.

quasi-political standing, the same objections do not apply in their case) and because representatives of the EEC's member-governments do not participate. From Canada's point of view, a commercial agreement, of the type pioneered by Yugoslavia and now adopted by Argentina, would be superior. It would provide for regular meetings of a ' commission mixte ' which may meet at whatever level is mutually agreed and would involve representation from member-states. This approach would require a formal agreement, a step which could be exploited to draw public attention to a government determination to enter into closer relations with the EEC. But the public and the press have as yet shown no interest in discussing options and the debate presumably is limited to the initiated in the government apparatus.

Lack of knowledge of the EEC as an institution is only one measure of Canadian ignorance and neglect of Europe. Another is the lack of interest shown in the Economic Commission for Europe, even though the government has been expending considerable efforts to achieve a close association with the Economic Commission for the Far East (ECAFE). Yet another important institution of the new Europe, still largely neglected, is the Council of Europe. In this instance the Council took the initiative of inviting the Canadian parliament to be represented at some of its deliberations and parliament has been quick to respond. But opportunities already utilized by non-European states, such as Australia and the United States, for associating themselves with some of the pioneering work of the Council—integrating social legislation, co-ordinating tourist regulations, developing legal conventions open to signature by non-members to give effect to these agreements—have been ignored by Canada. True, this pattern is not everywhere repeated. Canada co-operates fully in the work of the OECD, which has become the international focus for the consideration of many world economic problems. Canada still participates actively in NATO, which continues to be the instrument for Europe's defence, and which includes the newly formed Committee on the Challenges of Modern Society, active in environmental matters. Canada has over the years co-operated closely with individual European states in peacekeeping operations and has begun to collaborate in a comparable manner on development projects.

Apart from the bias of some Canadians against involvement with Europeans, tension with France has been an obstacle to any major governmental effort to seek increased Canadian connections with the new Europe. Canada's poor export performance during a period when competitor nations were doing much better suggests that Canadian businessmen have not been fully awake to opportunities in Europe. Only an effort dramatized by a personal visit by the prime minister to Western Europe, and in particular to the institutions of the new Europe—the EEC and the Council of Europe—could shake the lethargy and arouse the positive interest of government officials, businessmen, and private citizens. Yet it is impossible, given the events of the recent past, for Trudeau to visit Western Europe (Britain is still an exception) without including France—and until recently this has been inconceivable. Circumstances are changing, although with an election likely in Canada during the autumn of 1972, a visit to France would not be feasible until after that.

Trudeau has been aware of the importance to Canada of finding ways to balance the influence of the United States. Replying in 1968 to a journalist's question on Canadian–American relations in respect to foreign affairs, he stated:

Il est beaucoup plus dangereux pour le Canada de se voir bousculer par les Etats-Unis, que le contraire n'est dangereux pour ces derniers. Cela étant, je crois avantageux pour le Canada de s'intégrer dans un plus grand ensemble, que de rester, en tête-à-tête pot de terre en face du pot de fer.[13]

He continues to believe in the validity of the concept since he has represented Canada's increased contacts with the USSR as one way of ensuring as independent a foreign policy as possible for Canada. Europe is, by virtue of its power, past connections, and economic strength, the one region with which Canada might hope through sustained and purposeful effort so to increase the existing and substantial links as to diminish the crippling sense of dependency on the United States which Canadians at times feel. Europe could indeed be Canada's last chance. And from the European point of view, it could be a

[13] Pierre-Elliott Trudeau, *Réponses* (Montreal, 1968), p. 103.

matter of mutual assistance. Claude Julien has suggested that Canada, with its human, agricultural, and industrial resources, is the indispensable partner Europe needs to help it balance the hegemony of the United States: ' Mais pour l'Europe l'essentiel est de savoir si le Canada se laissera coloniser par les Etats-Unis ou si, au contraire, renforçant ses liens avec l'Europe, il l'aidera à équilibrer la puissance des Etats-Unis.'[14]

A major attempt to draw closer to Europe would require a considered decision by the government and a serious commitment of national effort—including the personal involvement of the prime minister. Relations with France have until recently made this impossible and still pose a considerable obstacle. Earlier, when the Trudeau government first took office, it was preoccupied with trying to decide whether to reduce Canadian forces in Europe. Once the decision had been taken to do so, Europe inevitably had to be portrayed as a region of diminished importance. Besides, at that time the government hoped that opportunities in countries across the Pacific and elsewhere in the third world would compensate for the diminished involvement in Europe. But this hope has not materialized and Canada's problem of how to live at ease with the United States in North America remains unresolved.

The challenge to Canada is how to escape the embrace of history. Its historical links with Europe, chiefly with Britain and to a much more limited extent with France, are an asset of depreciating value. The defence connection had great significance after the war but is now of declining importance. So Canada stands in a quandary—afraid to go ahead and accept North American continentalism which geography encourages, but reluctant in spite of old sentimental ties to work out realistic arrangements for a liaison with the new Europe.

[14] Julien, p. 15.

7

THE OUTER AREA

In his first foreign-policy statement as prime minister, Trudeau spoke critically of ' past preoccupations with Atlantic and European affairs '.[1] Later he suggested that increased attention should henceforth be paid to the third world: ' We're beginning to realize that countries like Japan, like China, like Australia, and those on the Pacific coast of South America, that these are as important partners for Canadians as the nations across the Atlantic '.[2] Inevitably an exception was made of the United States.

The policy review undertaken by the government has been a kind of test of Canada's opportunities in what the Duncan Report termed the ' Outer Area '.[3] For those who expected a total transformation of Canadian policy, the result has been a disappointment. It has revealed, in fact, that Canada's opportunities in the third world—except in the field of foreign aid—are limited, and the government has obviously been influenced by these conclusions.

New Window on Asia?

Trudeau had twice visited the Chinese People's Republic. In 1960 he stayed a month there and on his return wrote, with his travelling companion, Jacques Hébert, *Deux innocents en Chine rouge* (1961). In this book he had already expressed the opinion: ' que la politique des deux Chines est basée sur une ignorance profonde de la mentalité chinoise ' and concluded that the government of Mao Tse-tung ' sait que la question d'admettre la Chine aux Nations-Unis trouvera sa réponse avec le temps ' (p. 156). It was entirely natural, therefore, that in his first foreign-policy statement as prime minister he should have asserted that the government was proceeding immediately to

[1] Office of PM, press release, 29 May 1968.
[2] Office of PM, transcript of speech, Calgary, 12 Apr. 1969.
[3] Review Committee on Overseas Representation 1968–9, *Report*, Cmnd 4107 (1969), p. 57.

enter into negotiations with the government of China: ' Our aim will be to recognize the People's Republic of China Government as soon as possible and to enable that Government to occupy the seat of China in the United Nations, taking into account that there is a separate government in Taiwan '.[4] By January 1969 negotiations were already under way.

This decisiveness towards China ended two decades of Canadian uncertainty. In the spring of 1950 Canada had begun negotiations with the new communist Chinese government, seeking to avoid difficulties with which the British mission in Peking was faced. The Korean war put an abrupt stop to these discussions and it was not until the election of Diefenbaker in 1957 that a Canadian government was again ready to consider recognizing the People's Republic. Diefenbaker, reflecting the already prevalent Canadian view that the communist Chinese were the de facto rulers of China, was inclined to move towards recognition. As a preliminary step, he raised the subject when President Eisenhower visited Ottawa in July 1958, steeling himself for a protest on the merits of the proposition from J. F. Dulles, who was accompanying the president. But Eisenhower completely disarmed the prime minister by suggesting that China's admission to the UN would cause the United States to withdraw.[5] That seems to have ended Diefenbaker's interest in the question, because it was not again seriously considered until Pearson became prime minister.

There was in fact no forward movement during Pearson's government. In principle he favoured recognition, but events conspired against him without the United States having to make any overt move. Negotiations with the People's Republic over recognition while the United States was becoming increasingly embroiled in Vietnam would have been regarded by the Americans as an unfriendly act. China's own behaviour—the attack on India, followed by the cultural revolution and the publicized harassment of diplomats in China—also weakened the case for recognition. Thus Pearson was never presented with an obvious opportunity to begin negotiations.

---

[4] As n. 1.

[5] Private conversation with Norman Robertson, former under-secretary of state for external affairs.

By accident the timing of the election of the Trudeau government in June 1968 perfectly suited a move towards China. The United States was embarked on its halting withdrawal from Vietnam, and China's cultural revolution had gradually run its course. The government conducted the lengthy negotiations with skill, determination, and a clear objective. Delays there were as each side gradually felt out the other. The Chinese seemed to be particularly suspicious that Canada was promoting some kind of ' two-China ' policy on behalf of the United States. They were not prepared, as they had been with the French in 1964, to omit any reference to Taiwan in the memorandum of agreement. Canada for its part was determined not to define China's borders as including Taiwan, arguing that the act of recognition does not involve acceptance of all a state's border claims. The final formula, announced on 13 October 1970, constitutes a compromise acceptable to both sides, although the full Canadian position required elaboration in a supplementary statement by the secretary of state for external affairs, Sharp. The wording of the memorandum reads in part:

The Chinese government reaffirms that Taiwan is an inalienable part of the territory of the People's Republic of China. The Canadian government takes note of this position of the Chinese government. The Canadian government recognizes the government of the People's Republic of China as the sole legal government of China.

Sharp's supplementary statement elaborates, in terms which were discussed in advance with the Chinese, the Canadian position on Taiwan:

... From the very beginning of our discussions the Chinese side made clear to us their position that Taiwan was an inalienable part of Chinese territory and that this was a principle to which the Chinese government attached the utmost importance. Our position, which I have stated publicly and which we made clear to the Chinese from the start of our negotiations, is that the Canadian government does not consider it appropriate either to endorse or to challenge the Chinese government's position on the status of Taiwan. This has been our position and it continues to be our position. As the communiqué says, we have taken note of the Chinese government's view and we realize the importance they attach to it, but we have no comment to make one way or the other.[6]

[6] *External Affairs*, Nov. 1970, p. 378-9.

The objectives and impact of the French and Canadian decisions are interesting to compare. The French decision, reached in 1964, seems to have been taken to emphasize France's independence from the United States and its opposition to the Vietnam war. Subsequently, at the UN, the French gave their full support to the Albanian resolution (calling for the seating of the communist Chinese and the expulsion of the Nationalists) and also opposed the ' important question ' resolution which has since 1961 affirmed that a change in Chinese representation requires a two-thirds majority vote. France's action was not unusual, since this latter resolution has over the years been opposed by all states supporting the Albanian resolution except the United Kingdom.

Canada deliberately based its decision to exchange represent-ation with the People's Republic on an acceptance of the facts in China. No attempt was made to dramatize the decision. The United States, Japan, and other directly interested nations were kept informed of the process of negotiations. Subsequently, at the 25th session of the General Assembly, Canada voted for the ' important question ' resolution, making it clear however, that this was a transitional move to give the United States time to adjust to the new situation. Privately Secretary of State Rogers was advised at the time that in 1971 Canada would vote against the ' important question ' resolution.

A number of other states have followed the Canadian lead, but only in four instances, those of Italy, Belgium, Peru, and Lebanon, was the Ottawa formula for exchanging represent-ation with China actually used. In other cases the Chinese have not insisted on its repetition. It is evident that the good timing of the Canadian move and the low-key formula have done much to advance China's readmission into the world community, signified by its acceptance into the UN.

In purely bilateral terms, the full implications of the exchange of diplomatic recognition with China remain unclear. It is widely believed to have given Canada some edge in trade negotiations, particularly in competition with Australia for wheat sales. This advantage may prove to be short-lived, how-ever, as China finds other, more pressing, political criteria for trade decisions, or reacts against the very substantial imbalance of trade in Canada's favour. Recognition and the opening of a Peking mission have resulted in a general increase of interest and a flood of political, business, journalistic, and academic visitors from Canada, but a more open Chinese policy has had the same result in personal contacts with non-recognizing countries. It also saved Canada the embarrassment which some other allies of the United States have experienced as a result of the change in approach symbolized by Dr Henry Kissinger's surprise journey to Peking in July 1971. However, the most important result of Canada's recognition has probably been in the simple removal of a long-standing anomaly in Canadian foreign policy, and the simultaneous demonstration of Canadian initiative and sensible independence from the United States. Seen in this light by the vast majority of the Canadian public, the China tie is a tangible and popular foreign-policy achievement.

The favourable outcome of negotiations with China has dramatized the new Pacific orientation which Trudeau has sought to give to Canadian foreign policy. Public interest was further stimulated by the highly successful visit to China in July 1971 of Jean-Luc Pepin, minister of industry, trade and commerce, accompanied by a number of prominent businessmen. These successes have done more to promote a new Canadian awareness of its Pacific interests than has the government's policy review, one part of which was devoted to the Pacific. In fact, had the negotiations failed, the stress placed by the Trudeau government on developing Canadian relations with the Pacific would have seemed disproportionate.

In expanding its Pacific links with countries other than China Canada faces the problem that the areas of significant relationship are still confined primarily to trade, and then only with a few countries. In the policy review the government sought ways of giving more substance to these connections. Canada had already been a member of the Asian Development Bank for several years. It now proposed to seek closer association with ECAFE. An effort to achieve non-regional membership has been temporarily frustrated by opposition within the ECAFE secretariat, and the secretary of state for external affairs reported in the Standing Committee on External Affairs on 19

May 1971 that ' we are postponing ' consideration of the application for membership. However, the government has indicated that it retains its interest in ECAFE as a politically significant demonstration of increased interest in Asia, and that the effort to achieve membership or at least to extend its association will be renewed.

A growing field of Canadian involvement has been foreign assistance, although aid to date has been largely committed to India, Pakistan, and Malaysia, with Indonesia added as a new country of concentration in the last year.

The government has consciously considered and rejected a security role for Canada in the Pacific region. In this decision it undoubtedly has broad public support. Few Canadians consider that Canadian security interests are involved in the area. Canadian involvement in the Pacific in World War II was minimal. The participation in the Korean conflict of the early 1950s has always been treated by Canadians, not as a precedent, but as an exceptional UN peacekeeping episode, unlikely to be repeated. Involvement in the International Commissions for Supervision and Control in Indochina has been a continuing source of frustration to successive Canadian governments. Indeed experience in the Commissions with the intractable *troika*—India, Canada, and Poland—accounts in large measure for this government's assertion, in *Foreign Policy for Canadians*, that it would in future participate only ' where the peacekeeping operation and the Canadian contribution to it seem likely to improve the chances for a lasting settlement ' (p. 23).

As far back as 1958 frustration had led the Diefenbaker government to accede to Laotian pressure and withdraw the small Canadian mission in Laos, only to find that in 1961, preparatory to the 1962 Geneva agreement, the Commission had to be reconstituted and Canadian personnel sent back. Canadian representation in Laos has once again been reduced, this time to a token officer. In Cambodia the Commission has not operated since its withdrawal in December 1969, at Sihanouk's insistence, just before he fell from power. Only the Vietnam Commission maintains a semblance of operations, and this is mainly to preserve the principle of the Geneva Conference in case it could be useful in facilitating a peace settlement.

Inevitably this experience has left Canadians with little stomach for further peacekeeping in the region. The main advantage over the years—and an important tactical reason for maintaining the role in Vietnam—has been in providing an effective argument against any American suggestions, such as have been heeded by Australia, New Zealand, and Korea, for contributing forces to the war in Vietnam.

Canada has accepted peripheral involvement in other security problems of the Pacific region and the Indian subcontinent, partly through participation in peacekeeping operations and partly through military assistance. There have been Canadian contributions to two peacekeeping operations on the Indian–Pakistani border: one, set up as a result of the 1965 border conflict which began in the Rann of Kutch, was successfully wound up through Soviet mediation in Tashkent in January 1966; the other, over Kashmir, still continues, twenty-two years after its inception. There was another brief UN operation in West Irian in 1962–3 to cover the transfer of the territory from the Netherlands to Indonesia. The Commonwealth connection led to a more direct Canadian involvement in support of India in 1962 against the Chinese incursions, and in Malaysia in 1964 during the period of confrontation with Indonesia. But in both instances Canadian support was confined to the provision of limited amounts of military equipment, principally STOL transport aircraft, and related military training.

Canada is, despite these involvements, essentially detached from the security and political problems of the Pacific region. Nor is there any likelihood that the government's emphasis on a new orientation toward the Pacific will lead to changes here. But Trudeau, during the first of two major voyages to the Far East, spoke of the desire of the government to establish closer links with the countries of the Pacific rim. A conscious objective of both trips has been the stimulation of increased public interest, thereby to provide a reasonable foundation for the new Pacific orientation to Canadian foreign policy. In May 1970 the prime minister visited New Zealand, Australia, Malaysia, Singapore, Hong Kong, and Japan, a trip of seventeen days. In January 1971, en route to and from the Singapore Commonwealth Conference, he visited Pakistan, India, Indonesia, and

Ceylon, a trip of twenty-three days. That these were the first two extended foreign journeys by the prime minister indicates their symbolic significance.

These demonstrative activities are necessary because Canada has few traditional cultural and personal ties with Asia. Established immigrant populations have been relatively small. In 1941 there were 34,000 Chinese and 23,000 Japanese settled in Canada, and only in Vancouver were there sufficient concentrations of Asians to give them local importance. However, the situation is beginning to change. Immigration from Asia has increased markedly in recent years, particularly since the new non-discriminatory regulations were introduced by the Pearson government in 1967. In 1969, for instance, Asians—primarily Chinese, Indians, and Filipinos—represented 13 per cent of the total Canadian immigration figure.[7] These new Canadians will over time increase Canadian awareness and knowledge of the languages and cultures of Asia.

To speed this process, the policy review also announced plans to introduce several modest programmes, intended both to improve Canadian understanding of the area and to promote greater awareness of Canada among the governments and peoples of the region. These include schemes for supporting Asian studies in Canadian universities, making funds available for scholarships for study in the area, and establishing a Pacific Economic Advisory Committee.

The need for these programmes is undeniable, for in spite of some commercial and missionary contacts extending back into the nineteenth century, very few Canadians speak a major Asian language or have an understanding of any Asian culture. This, indeed, is the essential prerequisite for an extended Canadian involvement in the Pacific. Although *Foreign Policy for Canadians* was tabled in June 1970, there had been no follow-up a year and a half later on any of its specific proposals, with the one exception of the effort to develop a closer association with ECAFE. Unless the government is prepared to make available the modest resources needed to apply these programmes, the brave words about a new Pacific orientation will remain rhetoric. In this event, Canadian involvement in Asia

[7] Dept of Manpower & Immigration, *1969 Immigration Statistics* (1969), p. 21.

would be based fairly narrowly on reciprocal trade and investment and on the existing government programmes in the fields
of foreign assistance and immigration.

Japan

Japan is, of course, the focus of Canadian commercial and
investment interest in the region. As the following table shows,
Canada–Japan trade has grown at a phenomenal rate, to the
point where Japan may soon be Canada's second largest trading
partner, overtaking Britain if the rate of increase is maintained.

Canadian Trade with Japan ($ million)

Year	Exports	Imports
1960	178·6	110·4
1965	316·2	230·2
1969	624·8	495·7
1970	793·1	583·7

Sources: Speech by J.-L. Pepin, Vancouver, 20 May 1971; *Canada Year Book, 1964,
1968.*

It is perhaps worth noting, however, that although the dollar
balance may be in Canada's favour, the bulk of Canada's
exports move to Japan in the crudest form, while 96 per cent of
Japan's exports to Canada are *labour-intensive* processed and
manufactured goods. Japan has recently also become a substantial investor in Canada, particularly in the provinces of
British Colombia and Alberta. It has concentrated on providing
the financing for large-scale extractive projects, including the
related infrastructure such as transport, and offering a guaran-
teed long-term market. It is noteworthy that in general Japan
has followed the technique of Britain in the nineteenth century
and taken bonds rather than insisting on a controlling equity
position. Naturally this approach has been welcomed as one
less likely, particularly with Japan's lingering wartime reputation, to arouse fear of a Japanese take-over. But suspicions are
probably inevitable in any such arrangement, and some
Canadians worry that Japan could withdraw when the contracts have ended without suffering any losses.

Canadian interest in Japan has always been considerable.
When the Canadian government began hesitatingly in the inter-
war period to open diplomatic missions, the mission in Tokyo

was the fourth to be opened, after London, Washington, and Paris. That was in 1929. But contacts remained limited and rather formal. To cope with the growing volume of trade and investment, the two governments decided in 1962 to establish regular interministerial consultations of a kind which Canada had at the time only with Washington. Both bodies meet regularly and have become important instruments for reconciling major policy differences. By contrast, the only other comparable body, established with Britain in the mid-1960s, has rarely met, and a similar link with Mexico has been activated to consider the new US economic measures.

Australia

Australia is the other country in the Pacific region with which Canada has extensive contacts. These have been stimulated by the free movement of peoples and the important trading preference conveyed by the Commonwealth link. Australia also has shared with Canada the experience of having had consciously to turn from the United Kingdom to the United States as its primary source of security. However, the geographical isolation of Australia has meant that its experience has usually come some years later than that of Canada. Recently the Australians have begun to undergo the next stage in this chain of experiences, to discover the consequences of committing themselves uncritically to support of US policy in South-East Asia, only to find that the United States is moving rapidly towards withdrawal from Vietnam and seeking reconciliation with the People's Republic. These American moves may in future bring Canada and Australia much closer together in international politics, by removing what have been sources of irritation. For Australian governments, deeply and emotionally committed in Vietnam, have tended to regard Canada as shirking an international responsibility.

Canadian-Australian trade, while not impressive in absolute terms, is important to both countries. The flow is weighted heavily in Canada's favour and Australia is noteworthy as the overseas country which takes the highest proportion of its Canadian trade in manufactured products. It is also Canada's sixth largest market, ahead of major countries such as France,

Italy, and the USSR. Britain's entry into the Common Market will pose a special problem for the two countries, as this present basis for Commonwealth trade preferences will disappear. It can be assumed that Canada will seek to find some way of putting these preference arrangements on a bilateral basis.

There is some Canadian investment in Australia, mainly in mining and refining, which by 1970 amounted to about $400 million. This is, of course, a field where the two countries are in direct competition, though fortunately the world, and particularly the Japanese, market for industrial raw materials has been growing so rapidly that neither country has suffered yet from the other's action. Wheat is in a different situation, owing to the world surplus. Australia and Canada are both major exporters, and in recent years the competition has been intense. Selling problems, however, even when they have had important domestic repercussions, have not affected the favourable attitude of Canadians towards Australians, and others have been blamed for the problems. While the importance of residual ties of sentiment is undoubtedly declining on both sides, it is being replaced by a conscious awareness by Canadians and Australians of their common problems and interests in many fields. Australia could and should become a more important Canadian partner in the future.

India and Pakistan

Canada developed close ties with India during the first decade of that country's independence. The remarkable cordiality of this relationship is difficult to explain if account is taken of the distance separating the two countries and of their different economic conditions, social problems, and strategic circumstances. Nehru, speaking in 1954, at a banquet in Delhi, in honour of the Canadian prime minister, St Laurent, acknowledged the fact without throwing light on it when he spoke of ' a kind of kinship . . . [arising out of] some deeper kind of understanding '.[8]

This closeness seems to have derived much from the personal regard which Nehru and St Laurent had for each other. But

[8] D. C. Thomson, ' India and Canada: a decade of co-operation 1947–57 ', *Internat. Stud.* (Delhi), Apr. 1968, p. 420.

with the growth of membership in the multiracial Common-wealth and with the large increase in UN membership, both movements which started with Ghana's independence in 1957, the special importance of this relationship began rapidly to evaporate. One is tempted to suggest that the full measure of the change can be seen in the lack of a single mention of India or the subcontinent in *Foreign Policy for Canadians*. But then the policy papers were not intended to provide a comprehensive examination of Canadian interests abroad. The prime minister did visit India in January 1971, although he was careful to balance this with a shorter visit to Pakistan. Moreover, in 1962, when India came under attack from China, Canadian sym-pathy flowed strongly for India and tangible support followed. Finally, Canada is heavily committed to assisting Indian development: Canada is currently India's third most important source of development assistance, providing less than the United States but only slightly less than Britain; and the cumulative amount of Canadian aid represents nearly one-half of all bilateral aid so far provided by Canada. The conclusion which seems to emerge is that, although India no longer has for Canada the special importance it once had—and presumably vice versa—there remains a reservoir of sympathy and respect which can be of importance if unexpected problems arise.

Canada's relations with Pakistan have never achieved the same intimacy which Indo-Canadian relations have at times attained. Even so, Canada had committed itself as fully to Pakis-tan's economic development as it has to that of India. Recent events in East Pakistan, the flight of some ten million refugees into India, the war between India and Pakistan, Pakistan's defeat in East Bengal and the establishment of Bangladesh had threatened the peaceful development of the subcontinent, to which Canada had so heavily committed itself. Inevitably, therefore, Canada was interested in any settlement which would be viable over the longer term, and the government offered troops if a peace-keeping force had been needed to supervise a ceasefire acceptable to both India and Pakistan.

An informal parliamentary group had visited both countries in July 1971 and its report urged the government to increase its assistance not only to India but also to East Pakistan to avert a threatened food shortage. By November 1971 the government had allocated over $22 million—the third largest sum, after the United States and the United Kingdom—of aid to the Pakistani refugees from East Bengal then in India, and had directed that all its 1971 food aid allocation to Pakistan be distributed to East Pakistan. On the political level, the minister of external affairs, mindful of the criticism to which he had been subjected over Biafra, stated in the Commons on 16 June 1971 that 'the preferred settlement, of course, would be one in which those individuals who have been elected pursuant to the recent election in Pakistan should be given the responsibility of governing Pakistan, particularly East Pakistan'. This was a strong stand, anticipating the eventual recognition of Bangladesh, although this step was not taken until mid-February 1972, so as not to place unnecessary strain on Canada's future relations with Pakistan.

Latin America

Canadians should be beginning to feel that Latin America is the Cinderella of their foreign relationships. Trudeau came into office with this guilt complex and his 29 May 1968 press statement expressed a sentiment often heard before:

We have to take greater account of the ties which bind us to other nations in this hemisphere—in the Caribbean, Latin America—and of their economic needs. We have to explore new avenues of increasing our political and economic relations with Latin America where more than four hundred million people will live by the turn of the century and where we have substantial interests.

But Trudeau also promised a more concrete step; if re-elected he would send a ministerial mission to tour the region: ' This mission will be designed to demonstrate the importance the Government attaches to strengthening our bilateral relations with leading Latin American countries.'

The mission, duly dispatched, spent thirty days in October and November 1968 visiting eight countries. It included at various times five ministers and was led throughout by the secretary of state for external affairs. The delegation members, aware that similar missions in 1941, 1953, and 1958 had aroused unfulfilled expectations, were careful to try to avoid committing themselves. Sharp emphasized throughout that the delegation was on a ' voyage of discovery '.

Inevitably hopes were stimulated, not only in Latin America but also in Canada. The policy paper on Latin America therefore came as an anticlimax when it reiterated the main line of Canadian policy: to avoid joining the Organization of American States (OAS), while working for gradually increasing Canadian participation in the technical commissions of that body. But even before this, a more drastic confirmation of the government's approach was manifested in the list of diplomatic missions to be closed in 1969 as a result of an economy cut. Of 7 missions withdrawn, all of which had non-resident ambassadors, 3 were in Latin America—Uruguay, Ecuador, and the Dominican Republic—and a reduction of 16 members from the remaining 12 missions in Latin America, excluding the Commonwealth Caribbean, was effected.

The decision not to join the OAS was justified on traditional grounds:

. . . OAS membership might tend, at least initially, to restrict Canadian freedom of action in development assistance matters . . . [Another] result . . . would be the assignment, for financial reasons, of a lower priority to the development of any bilateral cultural programmes with Latin American countries. . . . [Further] the potential obligation to apply political and economic sanctions against another country by virtue of an affirmative vote of two-thirds of the members is a difficult feature of the OAS from the Canadian point of view.[9]

But the expressed intention to ' continue and intensify its participation in the work of various Pan-American and Latin American ' multilateral organizations has been pursued with greater determination than in the past. A Canadian representative attended the April 1971 meeting of the OAS General Assembly, which passed a resolution approving the principle of accrediting official observers. If this new constitutional arrangement is approved by the OAS Council—and the prospects are said to be good—Canada will then accredit a permanent observer mission to its headquarters in Washington. Depending

[9] *FPC: Latin America*, p. 22–3.

on the value of this experience, the Canadian government may well review the pros and cons of joining the OAS. In any case by 1968 Canada already belonged to, or participated in, many of the organizations and conferences, official and non-official, which together comprise the inter-American system. The policy paper announced the government's intention to seek full membership in four further official organizations, and to contribute to the Inter-American Emergency Assistance Fund.

Canadian trade with Latin America has never been large, and in a period of broadly expanding international trade, the relative percentage has remained static at about 3 per cent of total Canadian trade. Canadian investments are likewise small, so that Canada has been able to avoid the United States reputation for economic imperialism. There are, however, two important exceptions—Brazil and Guyana. The Brazilian Traction Light and Power Company (now known as Brascan) has investments in Brazil amounting to $567 million. This constitutes the largest single investment in Brazil, as well as being Canada's largest single overseas investment. Brascan has recently pursued a vigorous policy of attracting local investors and, with 150,000 Brazilian shareholders, it now has a strong local personality. Conditions in Guyana have not opened the same possibilities for local participation in the Aluminum Company of Canada's investment there. With assets valued at $130 million, its subsidiary, Demerara Bauxite Co. Ltd (Demba), represented a dominating force in that small country, and its taxes alone have provided 8 per cent of the ordinary revenue collected by the government. The Guyana government on 23 February 1971 nationalized Demba's holdings, and the Aluminum Company agreed on compensation of $53·5 million. Should Guyana fail to move against other foreign aluminium companies (notably Reynolds of the United States) on similar terms, the Canadian-based firm will claim discrimination, and governmental relations, which have until now been good, are likely to be affected.

The most important area of expanded Canadian interest in Latin America has been in the field of development assistance. For many years there was no bilateral programme of any kind in Latin America, although since the beginning of the century

Canadian missionaries in large numbers—especially from French Canada, where there has traditionally been a certain fraternal feeling towards Latin America—have been active there. Increasingly these men and women have become deeply involved in education and social work rather than in more traditional missionary work. There are now over 2,000 Canadian Roman Catholic missionaries in South America—mainly in Peru, Brazil, Chile, and Bolivia—and the contribution of these dedicated Canadians is, by all accounts, highly valued in all the countries in which they are active.

The first instrument through which Canada made an official and direct contribution to development in Latin America was the Inter-American Development Bank (IDB). Through an arrangement initiated in 1964, Canada has annually committed $10 million to be used for development loans. Being tied, however, has limited the effectiveness of this programme, and only about half the amount has so far been spent. Application was made in August 1971 for Canada to become a full and regular member of the IDB, and negotiations to this effect are under way.

The policy review led to the opening up of direct bilateral programmes primarily with Peru, North-east Brazil, Colombia, and the Central American region. The initial targets are modest, but this does constitute an important extension of Canadian involvement in Latin America and an entirely new area of official development-assistance activity. With the likelihood of an expanded aid budget, this programme should grow rapidly and could begin to extend significantly the degree of Canadian involvement in Latin America. There is reason, in fact, to believe that this could become both a more appropriate and a more distinctly Canadian link with Latin America than actual membership in the OAS.

Cuba

A separate word on Canadian relations with Cuba is justified because they have developed so differently from US-Cuban relations. Unlike the United States and all of the Latin American republics other than Mexico, Canada has maintained uninterrupted normal diplomatic relations with Cuba. Indeed, the

United States' use of the OAS as an instrument for exerting pressure on the member-states to break relations with Cuba was widely regarded in Canada as a reason for not joining that body. During the 1960s Canada's continued diplomatic relations with Cuba assumed a significant symbolic importance as a demonstration of Canadian independence from American influence in foreign policy. Canada has maintained fairly healthy trade relations with Cuba as well, although initially Canadian sales were limited to food and drugs in order not to give too much offence to the United States. Canada has also permitted landing rights to the Czechoslovak Air Lines en route to Cuba. Compensation was paid for Canadian firms and banks nationalized in Cuba. More recently, the Cuban authorities co-operated to the fullest extent possible in working out arrangements to receive and accept the kidnappers of James Cross in order to ensure his safe release.

The Caribbean

Closely linked geographically with Latin America, the newly independent countries of the Commonwealth Caribbean (and the remaining dependencies) have had different historical experiences and now have economies, social problems, and cultural backgrounds which are quite different from Latin America. They also differ widely from island to island which, along with their physical separation, impedes regional co-operation. This greatly complicates the problem for countries such as Canada which would like to deal at least with the Commonwealth Caribbean as a region. It can scarcely be done, as only individual contacts appear to be effective. For most countries this would be a reason for ignoring the whole area, but Canada's ties are too close and too old to make this possible.

Canadian contact with the British West Indies has developed out of a traditional exchange of sugar and molasses for cod. Trade was followed by investment, and Canadian banks and insurance companies have gradually acquired a dominant position in many of the islands. More recently, Jamaican and Guyanan bauxite and alumina have become the raw material source for Canada's aluminum industry. Canada is also a substantial importer of Trinidadian oil. Indeed, bauxite and oil have largely displaced in relative terms the traditional Canadian imports of sugar and citrus fruits.

With the rapid growth of tourism in the Caribbean, Canadians have become heavy investors in hotels and related facilities. As a result Canada is beginning for the first time in its history to attract the suspicion, the criticism, and even the hatred of local nationalists, an experience for which Canadians are totally unprepared. In Trinidad, where tension is already rife, the visit of the Governor-General, Roland Michener, in February 1969 was marred by demonstrations, prompted in particular by trials then taking place in Montreal of some black Caribbean students who had been prominently involved a few months before in the destruction of the computer centre at the Sir George Williams University in Montreal.

For historic reasons Canada's links have been mainly with the countries of the Commonwealth Caribbean, and this emphasis is likely to persist.[10] The special character of the link was dramatized in July 1966 by a conference in Ottawa, to which Pearson invited the prime ministers and premiers of the independent countries and major groups of dependencies. The conference confirmed the intention of the heads of participating governments ' to continue and strengthen the fruitful collaboration among them '[11] which had been begun in Ottawa. Canada agreed to make the Commonwealth Caribbean an area of concentration in its aid programme by committing $75 million over the succeeding five years, to undertake studies in the fields of air and sea transport with a view to opening up trade possibilities, and to find some means of improving the access of Caribbean sugar to Canada. In the years which followed the specific undertakings were carried out to the letter. A special rebate scheme on sugar imports was introduced, under which the duty collected was returned to the treasuries of the exporting countries; and the studies were undertaken. The aid target was surpassed within four years and in fact Canadian aid surpassed British aid allocations to the region. In per capita terms, the

[10] Haiti, owing to its use of French, could prove to be an exception, although as long as President Duvalier (senior) was in power, the only regular link, apart from a substantial Canadian missionary community, has been a small stream of immigrants anxious to escape the poverty and repression.

[11] Parl. Senate, Standing Ctte on For. Aff., *Canada-Caribbean Relations* (1970), p. 3.

figures are more impressive, amounting to US$8·80 in 1969–70 for Barbados, the Little Seven,[12] and British Honduras, US$6·30 for Guyana, US$4·89 for Trinidad and Tobago, and US$2·64 for Jamaica—all far greater than the next highest allocation in Canada's programme, US$0·84 to Ghana.[13]

But if the letter of the 1966 conference was followed, the spirit was not. The Caribbean premiers began increasingly to question whether the meeting had led to greater collaboration.. Then in March 1970 a Canadian decision to withdraw the sugar rebate was publicly announced. In its place Canada offered a $5 million contribution to an agricultural development fund to assist in the modernization of agriculture. Although Caribbean officials had been informed of these proposed changes, there had been no interministerial consultations. At a meeting (already scheduled) in Kingston, Jamaica, the week following the Canadian public announcement, the premiers expressed their anger in a strong statement which stated that the affected governments

1. Deprecate the unilateral termination of the 1966 Ottawa Agreement.

2. Do not consider the proposed Agricultural Development Fund as a substitute for the rebates which accrued to the benefit of the Sugar Industry of the Commonwealth Caribbean countries.

3. Firmly resist the erosion of the preferences already granted by Canada to the Commonwealth Caribbean countries on the importation of sugar.[14]

The Canadian government, which had been divided over the decision to withdraw the rebate, moved quickly, reinstating the rebate temporarily and sending the former secretary of state for external affairs, Senator Paul Martin, on an extended mission of inquiry which took him to all the Commonwealth Caribbean countries. The mission appears to have been a success and the sugar rebate has been extended for a further year. But the main reason for success was probably the renewal of contact at the political level. As a report by the Senate's

[12] Antigua, Dominica, Grenada, Montserrat, St Kitts-Nevis-Anguilla, St Lucia, St Vincent.

[13] As n. 11, p. 25.

[14] *International Canada* (Toronto), Apr. 1970, p. 91.

Standing Committee on Foreign Affairs, issued prior to Martin's visit in June 1970, affirmed:

it is unmistakably clear that the full and frank exchange of views essential to real partnership has not been achieved. . . . The expectations of 1966 can still be realized and the Canada-Caribbean partnership can function if all concerned now show a readiness to continue the kind of close consultation initiated at that time.

However, as the same report observed:

In view of the distinct trends within the area Canada can expect continuing and even growing criticism and hostility from some sectors of opinion in the Caribbean. Persistent efforts will be required to keep this situation in perspective and forestall excessive reactions on the part of the Canadian public or other damaging effects on good mutual relations.[15]

Africa and the Commonwealth

One of the most controversial statements in *Foreign Policy for Canadians* was a passage which spoke of disenchantment and belittled Canada's past role as mediator. Noting the risk in postulating a specific role for Canada, the policy paper suggested that:

It is even riskier—certainly misleading—to base foreign policy on an assumption that Canada can be cast as the ' helpful fixer ' in international affairs. That implies . . . a reactive rather than active concern with world events, which no longer corresponds with international realities or the Government's approach to foreign policy (p. 8).

The strength of feeling conveyed by these sentences derives from the reaction in official circles to the exaggerated public expectations of Canada's international influence which had developed before Trudeau's accession.

While the Trudeau government was right to deflate this balloon of expectations, the job was too well done because the impression has been widely conveyed that the role of mediator was not a fit one for Canada. This ignores the genuine contributions which Canada and Mr Pearson personally had made in this role in the past. It also overlooks Canada's continuing special fitness and aptitude for the role. As Dr K. Holsti, an

[15] As n. 11, pp. xiii, xiv.

academic witness before the Commons Committee on External Affairs and National Defence, stated, roles cannot always be self-determined:

Roles have to be seen also in terms of the expectations of other governments. It is not just a question of a government saying we will play this role or that role, it is a question also of what kinds of opportunities and expectations other governments expect you to undertake. I think we can certainly see in the present set of circumstances that there are a number of voices emanating from Africa who are arguing that because of certain policies undertaken by the British there is definitely a role for Canada vis-à-vis the Commonwealth.[16]

It was to the credit of the Canadian government that when the government of Edward Heath announced that it felt free to resume arms sales to South Africa under the terms of the Simonstown Agreement and thereby threatened to break up the Commonwealth, Trudeau was prepared and ready to act as mediator—in spite of the rejection of the ' helpful fixer ' role. It was doubly ironic that the first time this role should have been thrust on the present Canadian government should have occurred over a Commonwealth problem. For the Commonwealth had been largely ignored in the policy review, and the sparse references were even defended by the secretary of state for external affairs: ' I think [the brief mention] does reflect the reality of the world . . . that the Commonwealth is now not a policy-making body and it isn't a trade promotion organization. It is a place where we can meet with countries with some sort of common links with the past.'[17]

The Canadian government's efforts to head off a crisis on arms sales were not inconsiderable. They began with a strong private protest delivered as soon as the British government's new policy was announced. This protest was somehow leaked to the press in London, causing some unfortunate tension in Anglo-Canadian relations. In the face of Heath's unyielding determination, some black African states began to threaten to boycott the Singapore meeting. It seemed that the Commonwealth might break up without even a conference being held

---

[16] *Mins of Proc. & Evidence*, 19 Jan. 1971, p. 9.
[17] CBC-TV interview, 26 June 1970.

to consider the issue in dispute. The Canadian government moved fast. The prime minister sent his assistant in the field of foreign affairs, Ivan Head, to talk to Presidents Nyerere and Kaunda and to persuade them to attend the conference. Coincidentally the British were urged to take no overt step until the conference had met. The conference did take place, with Trudeau's encouragement a compromise formula was worked out, and—in spite of a minor sale of helicopters which may have satisfied political pressures in the United Kingdom— another confrontation may have been avoided.

This Canadian intervention was entirely in the tradition of the past. Nowhere in fact had this mediatory role been more apparent than in the continuing effort to hold the Commonwealth together—Diefenbaker at the 1960 Commonwealth Conference in London which led to South Africa's withdrawal, Pearson in 1966 at the Lagos Conference when the NIBMAR formula which was intended to cope with Rhodesian independence was worked out.[18]

Why has Canada exerted so much effort in this continuing endeavour to hold the Commonwealth together? Is it a proclivity for role playing or is a Canadian interest involved? An important clue may lie in a little-noticed statement by Trudeau on his return from the Commonwealth Prime Ministers' Conference held in London in January 1969. The prime minister spoke glowingly of the strengths and advantages of the Commonwealth:

. . . This is perhaps the greatest strength of the Commonwealth, this opportunity on a regular basis for men of good will to sit down together and discuss with one another the problems which affect them and the 850 million people they represent.

. . . . The Commonwealth is an organism not an institution—and this fact gives promise not only of continued growth and vitality but also of flexibility as well.

. . . . The Commonwealth conference is a forum for men who are as different as God has made them. It is a meeting place where men are able to demonstrate the advantage of dissimilarity, the richness of diversity, the excitement of variety.

[18] *The Economist*, 15 Jan. 1966.

.... For these reasons, Mr Speaker, I assured the London conference that Canada firmly supported the Commonwealth principle.[19]

This statement stands in striking contrast with the negative remarks of the secretary of state cited above and the brief attention in the policy papers. How can these contrasting positions be reconciled? The prime minister's statement suggested that he sees the Commonwealth mainly as an organ for personal diplomacy. It is certainly significant that in crises involving the Commonwealth he has sent Ivan Head as a personal emissary rather than using officials of the Department of External Affairs.

While the prime minister's personal interest can account for the effort expended in trying to hold the Commonwealth together, this does not represent a Canadian interest. However, with the growing confrontation over arms sales to South Africa in the summer and autumn of 1970, it became apparent in Canada that there was widespread concern at what a Commonwealth break-up might mean. The government, probably to its surprise, found itself being pressed on the domestic front to affirm that it would not withdraw, no matter whether some African states were to do so, and was even urged to offer to step in in Britain's place if Britain withdrew. No obvious explanation emerged for this interest, but it was widespread and genuine enough to persuade the government that vigorous efforts to save the Commonwealth would avoid the more difficult choices to be made if it disappeared.

Nigeria

The phenomenal public interest in the fighting which resulted from Biafra's efforts to secede from Nigeria has defied rational explanation. Why did the suffering of the wounded, the displaced, and the starving in this civil war arouse so much more public concern than have comparable conflicts in Yemen, South Sudan, Chad, and Indonesia? One can point to some special factors—good publicity by the Biafrans, including considerable television coverage, and long-established links with the major Christian churches—but these will not explain why the response in some Western countries was stronger than in

[19] H. of C.Deb., 20 Jan. 1969, p. 4461.

others. Canada's was in any case one of the strongest, and the opposition parties, both of the left and of the right, made effective use of this issue to attack the government. For several months they had the government on the run, and the secretary of state for external affairs, Mitchell Sharp, found himself in great difficulty.

This issue caught fire in Canada very soon after Trudeau's new government had taken office. During an informal and accidental press conference in the garden of his official residence, in August 1968, the prime minister responded in a half-joking manner that he did not know where Biafra was. (Joking because he had in fact visited Iboland while he was teaching at a Canadian World University Service seminar in West Africa in 1957.) Although parliament had been prorogued at the time, the very first question addressed to the prime minister when the new parliament opened on 12 September was on Biafra, and this topic continued to be the primary focus of daily questioning during the session. The secretary of state for external affairs bore the brunt of the attack. Having just taken over the portfolio, he was unfamiliar with the subject and had not yet gained confidence in his advisers. His replies at first showed some indecisiveness on the principle of intervention, which suggests that he was not fully persuaded by the advice he was receiving that the African states were opposed to any international intervention. This hesitancy disappeared after he went to the General Assembly and had a chance to ascertain African views for himself.

Many traditional supporters of the UN in Canada were disturbed by the organization's unwillingness to act as an agency for sending relief to Biafra and for mediating that conflict. The UN had taken its cue from the Organization of African Unity, where the great weight of opinion supported the federal Nigerian government in order to preserve the principle of territorial unity against the threat of balkanization. Frustrated by the UN's refusal to take action and by the emphasis of article 2 (7) of the Charter regarding non-intervention in internal affairs, a number of concerned Canadians began to speak in favour of a higher right to come to the aid of suffering humanity in Biafra: ' There is also a long-term need to organize an international community which would be able to intervene even in civil wars to preserve human rights and lives. We cannot afford in this world to experience tragedies like Biafra.'[20]

The opposition pressed particularly for government support of the private relief efforts which were flying in supplies to Biafra from the neighbouring Portuguese island of São Tomé. Sharp was emphatic but strangely imprecise in opposing these proposals. Rumours began to circulate that the prime minister was disappointed in his minister and would drop him. Other ministers showed signs of wanting his job, all of which whetted the appetite of the opposition. It is difficult to be confident about the forces then agitating the Liberal government, but there appears to have been a school of thought within the cabinet which argued that a government which emphasized the need for public participation in the process of government should accede to public pressure so obviously manifest in the Biafran case. In short, the cabinet was divided, with Sharp arguing the case for realism: that Nigeria would eventually win; that if Canada wished to maintain good relations with Nigeria it would have to support the federal government; that the principle of territorial unity had to be maintained in Africa; that Canadian relations with black Africa could be compromised if aid were given to Biafra; and that Canada as a federal state with its own internal problems should fully support the federal power in Nigeria. So the debate continued, constituting the dominant international issue in Canada throughout the autumn of 1968. Within the cabinet a parallel debate proceeded with questions of substance heightened by the natural rivalries within a new government and by the fact that the prime minister had not yet declared himself personally.

The prime minister took his first initiative in October 1968, when he sent his personal assistant, Ivan Head, to visit General Gowon. The aim was to work out some means acceptable to the federal government of flying in relief supplies to Biafra,[21] which was the sensitive point in the Canadian public debate. But

[20] Andrew Brewin, MP: ibid., 12 Jan. 1970, p. 2211.
[21] Canadian military transport aircraft had flown three missions to Biafra from São Tomé in August 1968 before disagreements between the federal Nigerian government and the Biafran authorities over the conditions of flight led to their termination.

protracted efforts, including second and third visits by Head in June and December 1969, failed to find workable arrangements acceptable to the two sides. Then suddenly, on 9 January 1970, the government announced that it was willing to provide financial relief to Canairelief, the Canadian voluntary organization established to fly supplies into Biafra. Just as unexpectedly, two days later, Colonel Ojukwu announced the surrender of Biafra and fled to a neighbouring country. The Canadian government had clearly been caught by surprise and hastily backtracked on its reversal of position in order to maintain its standing with the Nigerian government. The effort was successful and Canadian relations have since become established on a very strong basis. Indeed the standing of the Canadian government with other African states was preserved and enhanced by the general Canadian policy of non-involvement in African affairs. But no one was more relieved by the outcome than the Canadian secretary of state for external affairs, who thereby gained his first respite since taking office.

South Africa

Canada's policies toward South Africa have come under increasing scrutiny and criticism within the country from a number of relatively small, but articulate and well-informed groups. Canada has over the years conformed with almost all the responsible UN resolutions regarding Portuguese colonies, Rhodesia, South-West Africa and South Africa. In the autumn of 1970, in line with a recent resolution, the sale of spare parts for some weapons sold to South Africa a decade earlier were cut off.

In December 1971, during a one-day visit to Ottawa, Heath informed Trudeau in detail of the British government's proposal for achieving a settlement with Rhodesia. Trudeau declined to take any position on the proposal, but took an immediate decision to send his assistant, Ivan Head, on another exploratory mission to black Africa. His task was to seek the opinions of Nyerere, Kaunda, and Gowon, so that Trudeau could take their views into account before making up his mind on the British proposal.

Canada, like Britain and many of the countries of Western

Europe, has a considerable range of contacts from investment to tourism with South Africa. Perhaps for this reason the government's policy has been ambivalent.

The reaction of Canadians [to the South African problem] has two main characteristics. One is a broad revulsion against the racial discrimination . . . and a general agreement that self-determination for Africans is a principle that cannot be denied. . . . The other is the reaction of businessmen who see better-than-normal opportunities for trade and investment. . . . The Canadian Government's attitude can be seen as reflecting two policy themes which are divergent in this context: (1) Social Justice and (2) Economic Growth. . . . The Government has concluded that Canadian interests would be best served by maintaining its current policy framework . . . which balances two policy themes of importance to Canadians.[22]

This argument has aroused the government's critics to protest by issuing a ' black paper ' on South Africa. Subsequently, when the Commons Standing Committee on External Affairs organized a meeting in June 1971 to hear witnesses on Southern African issues, eight groups, including the YWCA, Canada University Service Overseas, and the United Church[23] asked to be heard. While the activity of these critical groups has until recently been directed primarily at the government, they are now widening their range, engaging in public education, and directly challenging companies trading in the region. A particularly massive effort is being directed against the sale of aluminum ingot to Portugal for use in the Caborra Bassa Dam project in Mozambique. About forty persons bought shares or were named as proxies by the YMCA and attended —and very much disrupted—the 1971 annual meeting of the Aluminum Company of Canada, carrying their challenge to the heart of corporate power.

The government can expect continuing pressure on this front. There are no correspondingly articulate and committed advocates of the other side, although business interests will resist if the government starts seriously to restrict normal trade. For the moment the critics are not advocating an embargo and

---

[22] *FPC: United Nations*, pp. 19–20.

[23] The United Church of Canada was formed in June 1925 from members of the Congregational Church of Canada, the Methodist Church of Canada, and the Presbyterian Church in Canada and the local Union Churches in Western Canada.

are limiting themselves to pressing for an end to anomalies such as the continued benefit to South Africa from the Common-wealth preference, as a direct result of which almost one-quarter of Canada's sugar supplies are coming from South Africa (double the amount from the Caribbean countries, to which Canada is supplying large quantities of aid).

Black Africa

Canada's contacts with the countries of black Africa have developed rapidly in the decade since their independence. In the past virtually the only link was through missionary activity which, as in Latin America, was widespread and has contri-buted broadly to the social and intellectual development of the countries in which they were active. Currently there are over 2,200 Canadian Catholic missionaries, primarily concentrated in Cameroon, Malawi, the Zaïre Republic (Congo Kinshasa), Lesotho, Madagascar, and Uganda.

Aid is overwhelmingly the major component of the present relationship with black Africa. Canada has also provided some military assistance to Ghana, Nigeria, and Tanzania. Trade has been non-existent and even today it consists almost entirely of goods moving through the aid stream. With francophone Africa the dispute over Quebec's role in foreign affairs has added an extra dimension to the relationship. A special kind of sympathy has developed with Commonwealth Africa owing primarily to Canada's role as an intermediary and to the support given in times of emergency, for example, the military transport aircraft provided in 1965 to fly oil to Zambia after the Rhodesian embargo. President Julius Nyerere emphasized this link when receiving an honorary degree at the University of Toronto in 1969: ' We believe that this country [Canada] has both the opportunity and the willingness to try to build bridges in the world and, in particular, to build a bridge across the chasm of colour '.[24]

The rapid development of Canada's contacts with the countries of black Africa is transforming the situation facing Canadian policy-makers. However, the lack of genuine trade with black Africa accounts for the desire of the government not

[24] *Stability and Change in Africa* (Dar es Salaam, 1969), p. 141.

to let action against South Africa's racist policies interfere with that trade. In fact Canada and Australia are the only two developed countries whose trade with South Africa is greater than is their combined trade with black Africa. In Canada's case the government's reticence is further increased because the balance of trade is highly favourable to Canada (in 1970 exports of $104 million as against imports of $45 million) and a significant portion of these exports is in labour-intensive manufactured goods. By contrast with the United Kingdom, however, Canada's investments are small, and more than 50 per cent are in the hands of one company (George Weston Ltd).

It is difficult to anticipate the consequences of the clash of the two principles of social justice and economic growth, but the Trudeau government has shown itself sensitive to charges of ignoring social justice. Should pressure within Canada for action against South Africa continue to grow, and should contacts with the countries of black Africa increase as they have in the past decade, it is probable that Canada's official ties with South Africa will diminish and that they will grow correspondingly with the countries north of the Zambesi.

8

THE IDEALIST IMPULSE

THE Trudeau government came to office anxious to remove the grounds for ' public disenchantment ' with Canadian foreign policy. This was a highly self-conscious process:

We Canadians found a lot to be proud of in 1967 and also some things to question. Above all we became keenly aware in our centennial year that significant changes . . . have taken place in the world around us and within the body politic of our own nation. We found ourselves questioning longstanding institutions and values, attitudes and activities, methods and precedents which have shaped our international outlook for many years. We found ourselves wondering whether in the world of to-morrow Canada can afford to cling to the concepts and role casting which served us in our international endeavours of three decades or more.[1]

The government has been remarkably successful in adjusting to policies so as to remove issues which had aroused strong criticism and in introducing in their place changes which command wider support. But it has not had similar success in restoring an overall sense of public purpose to Canadian policy. It is undeniable, as a recent American study has suggested, that Canada has suffered ' loss of a sense of destiny as a *middle power* in world affairs '.[2]

The government's dilemma derives from its decision, evident in *Foreign Policy for Canadians*, that to remedy the deficiencies of the past, it had to attack the undifferentiated idealism which had marked Canadian international activity in recent years. This necessarily involved preaching the doctrine of national interest. Just as inevitably, such an emphasis has downgraded the idealist impulse—the essential basis for a sense of public purpose. While the government, through the increased support it has given to foreign aid, has in practical terms set policy on a

[1] Office of PM, press release, 29 May 1968.
[2] W. P. Kintner & R. L. Pfaltzgraff, Jr., *Soviet Military Trends: implications for US security* (Washington 1971).

direction susceptible of arousing idealistic feelings, it has hesitated to undertake the long-term commitment and set goals, without which no policy can have a larger meaning.

The UN

In intellectual and in practical terms the UN has provided the idealistic basis for postwar Canadian foreign policy and Canadian public support for the UN is unusual by the standards of most nations. Even participation in NATO has always been justified with an assertion that Canada would have preferred to entrust its security to the UN, but that in view of the latter's inadequacies NATO had to be created. The UN was the scene of some of Pearson's greatest diplomatic triumphs. Political support for the organization has always been carefully nurtured. The Canadian delegation to the first General Assembly included leaders of all parties and, although this practice was not repeated, it has been superseded by a practice of attaching half a dozen MPs on a rotating basis as observers throughout the Assembly. In fact, as one commentator has observed, ' exceptional support for international organizations . . . became the chief distinguishing feature of Canada in its post-1945 external relations '.[3]

The Trudeau government, while not changing any specific policies, gives the impression of being less UN-oriented than its predecessors. In his opening address to the 24th Assembly in 1969, Mitchell Sharp warned of the serious institutional problems facing the Organization:

. . . Canada believes that the United Nations must fail to reach its goals if it cannot come to grips with its own problems. . . . The UN (including all its organs and associated agencies) is drowning in a sea of words. . . . This has led governments to attach less importance to the United Nations' activities and efforts. . . . Member nations, locked in outdated conceptions of sovereignty and national interest, find debate to be a convenient substitute for action.[4]

The prime minister declined the opportunity to speak first in the twenty-fifth anniversary debate and could not be persuaded that his appearance in the General Assembly would

[3] P. Lyon, in *Internat. J.*, Winter 1970–1, p. 22.
[4] Dept of External Affairs, *Statements and Speeches*, 29 Sept. 1969.

have symbolic importance to Canadians as a demonstration of the government's continuing commitment to the UN. It was probably his own experience at the UN in 1966 which strengthened his decision not to contribute to the anniversary debate, although the kidnapping crisis, which had just begun, provided the immediate justification for his withdrawal. The impression of a new Canadian reticence towards the UN is, nevertheless, difficult to confirm, because in two specific respects the government has chosen to extend its involvement: it has increased from 20 to 25 per cent the proportion of Canadian official aid to be dispensed through multilateral organizations, most of which belong to the UN family, and it has given strong support to the Conference on the Environment to be held in Stockholm in 1972. The attitude is perhaps best revealed in the cautious assertion in *Foreign Policy for Canadians* that ' membership in international organizations is not an end in itself and Canada's effort at all times will be directed to ensuring that those organizations continue to serve a useful purpose to the full extent of their capacity to do so ' (p. 29).

The UN's activity which has brought Canadians the greatest satisfaction has been peacekeeping. Canada's military capacity, its uncommitted international posture, its proximity to UN headquarters, the international reputation for trust it enjoyed, and its willingness to serve had all contributed to its being invited to participate in virtually all UN peacekeeping operations. In the late 1950s and early 1960s it seemed that the UN had discovered in peacekeeping an opportunity, beyond the cold war, to contribute to international security and Canada, as a major contributor, to have found an international role for which it was ideally fitted. Between 1960 and 1965 five peacekeeping missions with Canadian participation were established, and in 1964 the Pearson government organized a major international conference of peacekeeping specialists. But inherent weaknesses—problems of financing, the reluctance of Afro-Asian nations to involve outside powers, inadequacies in the UN secretariat—frustrated peacekeeping, and since 1965 not one new force or observer mission has been approved or even seriously considered.

Public support for peacekeeping persists in Canada in spite

of disappointments. The abrupt expulsion of the UNEF force from Gaza in 1967 came as a severe shock to government and public alike. That a Canadian contingent was involved was probably less of a blow than what the incident revealed of the UN's inability to resist Nasser's demand in a situation which was so obviously explosive. The coincidence that Pearson, the innovator of UNEF, was prime minister at the time of expulsion naturally intensified the government's anguish.

Canadian attitudes to UN peacekeeping have always been highly idealistic. Unlike the Scandinavian countries, which have tempered their contributions to UN forces by requiring full compensation for all personnel, Canada has absorbed most direct costs for units it has provided to successive peacekeeping operations. However, the business-like approach of the Scandinavians has cushioned them from disappointment over the UN reverses and failures in peacekeeping which Canadian generosity has not afforded Canada.

The government has accepted that the high tide of UN peacekeeping has passed, at least for the present. The 1971 White Paper on Defence concludes that ' for many reasons the scope for useful and effective peacekeeping activities now appears more modest than it did earlier, despite the persistence of widespread violence in many parts of the world '. In spite of this sober conclusion, the government has decided to ' maintain its capability to respond quickly [and] a battalion group . . . will remain on stand-by . . . for service within peacekeeping bodies '.[5]

The Canadian public has been reluctant to face up to the ending of this role which had contributed so much to Canada's international reputation. Only the shock of the UNEF expulsion gained wide notice. That no peacekeeping missions have been set up since 1965 has provoked little speculation on the UN's future in this field. The measure of the Canadian public's continued faith can be judged from this ringing affirmation by a Commons Committee report in 1970 on the UN and peacekeeping:

The need for our continuing and active support for [peacekeeping] has not diminished with the passage of time. For Canada now to lose

5 *Defence in the 70s*, pp. 5, 40.

heart, and reduce its interests in peacekeeping would be an abdication of responsibility. No other country could fill the gap thus opened—and the development of peacekeeping would be set back with incalculable, but certainly disastrous effect.[6]

Canadians still instinctively turn first to the UN when international action is required. There is undeniably a Canadian prejudice in its favour, an attitude strengthened by the fact that no important Canadian interest has been challenged or attacked in the organization. But with the disappearance of frequent opportunities for contributing to international stability through peacekeeping, Canadians have lost a major outlet for their idealism and an important support for national identity.

Development assistance

It is in the field of development assistance that the Trudeau government has chosen to make its major international effort. This emphasis on external aid was apparent in the first major speech Trudeau made after becoming prime minister. On 13 May 1968, in Edmonton, Alberta, he spoke at length of the great disparity between rich and poor nations and of the need for expanded development assistance, stressing the humanitarian aspect, the potential benefits Canada would derive, and quoting Pope Paul VI's assertion that ' the new name for peace is development '.

The newly appointed president of the Canadian International Development Agency (CIDA) espressed an intention and an aspiration of the government when, speaking in 1971, he envisaged for Canada: ' the task of playing a significant, if not a leading role in developing a new international community with a different set of values, as expressed in terms of national expenditure, from the values accepted today '.[7] Development assistance is consciously seen, not only as being useful in itself, but also as providing a new role where, with the weakening of US will, Canada can set an example internationally and at the same time implement a policy which cannot be criticized as being a pale reflection of the Americans.

This search for identity and for exercising some kind of

[6] SCEAND, *8th Report*, 1969, p. 21.
[7] SCEAND, *Mins of Proc. & Evidence*, 4 Feb. 1971, p. 16.

world leadership seems to be a part of the Canadian psyche. Escott Reid, one of the principal Canadian architects of the NATO concept and now a senior adviser in CIDA, has argued that:

If Canada were to double its present defense expenditures of 1·8 billion Canadian dollars a year, this would increase the total expenditures of the NATO countries by 1½ per cent. But if Canada were to increase its net expenditures on foreign aid to poor countries by 1·8 billion Canadian dollars a year, this would increase the total net expenditures of the wealthy white countries on foreign aid to poor countries by 33 per cent. . . . Canada would become one of the two leading countries in the world in the struggle against world poverty. . . . [8]

The Trudeau government has moved concretely in this direction, albeit with characteristic prudence. Canadian foreign-assistance appropriations were increased in 1971–2 by 16·5 per cent and in 1972–3 they will probably be increased by a further 16 per cent to an annual total of $492 million. While the government has accepted the goals of the Commission on International Development,[9] it has not accepted the 1975 target. However, if the present rate of increase were to be maintained or slightly increased the target of 0·7 per cent of GNP in official aid by 1975 could be reached in the 1975–6 appropriations. It is ironic that the Pearson government in 1967 committed itself, apparently without calculating the full implications, to the attainment of the 1 per cent target for aid from all sources by the end of that decade. Yet in relative terms disbursements for official aid actually declined during the final years of the Pearson government, dropping from 0·33 per cent of GNP in 1966 to 0·26 per cent in 1968.[10] Trudeau is determined not to make idle promises and, knowing the tremendous pressures on scarce financial resources which can be generated in a federal state, has decided that it is wise not to arouse false expectations and then fail to satisfy them.

The Canadian performance in the field of official aid has

[8] 'Canada and the struggle against world poverty', *Internat. J.*, Winter 1969–70, pp. 146 & 147.
[9] The chairman of this Commission, set up by the World Bank in 1967, was the former prime minister, Lester Pearson.
[10] OECD, *1970 Review: Development assistance* (1970), p. 181.

improved markedly in the two years since 1968, and it is by this target that the government wants its performance to be judged. Being a capital importing country, it is not feasible for Canada to become a large investor in developing countries and there is no prospect of Canada attaining the 1 per cent target of official and private transfers. Indeed the special position of Canada is recognized within the UN aid community. The development strategy officially endorsed by the General Assembly, in setting the 1 per cent target, makes a special exception (known as the Canadian clause): ' having regard to the special position of those countries which are net importers of capital '.[11]

The Canadian government has been making serious efforts not only to increase the size of its development assistance appropriations but also to improve their quality. The 1970 policy paper on development assistance [12] had the following specific provisions:

(a) reduction in the proportion of bilateral aid tied to Canadian procurement from an average of 66 per cent to as low as 53 per cent; [13]

(b) shipping costs no longer to be regarded as local costs and therefore CIDA can cover these costs if necessary;

(c) the proportion of Canadian official aid for distribution through multilateral channels to be increased to 25 per cent;

(d) increased support of the private sector's participation in the development programme.

In addition to these specific provisions, CIDA has been making apparently successful efforts to improve the administration of Canadian aid. In past years CIDA has consistently failed to spend its full appropriations and has built up large balances. For, in contrast with other government departments whose unspent appropriations must be transferred to the consolidated revenue fund at the end of the fiscal year, CIDA has been allowed to accumulate its unexpended funds. However, the

[11] UN, *International Development Strategy: Action programme of the GA for the 2nd UN development decade* (1970), p. 9.

[12] *FPC: International Development.*

[13] Soon after taking office the Trudeau government had reduced Canadian procurement from 80 to 66 per cent.

growing amounts carried forward had become a source of embarrassment. For the first time in 1971 expenditures have equalled appropriations of the preceding year and this problem seems now on the way to being overcome.

Likewise over the last few years a policy of consolidation has been attempted, but with less success. Canadian aid used to be dispersed in a random way; indeed at one time Canada had aid programmes in more countries than did the United States. Now the government has announced that it ' intends to allocate the major portion [in the order of 80 per cent] of Canadian bilateral funds to selected " countries of concentration ", and to specialize in assisting particular sectors within those countries in which Canada has special competence '.[14] This objective is a good one. In the words of the report on international development assistance of the House of Commons Standing Committee on External Affairs and National Defence, ' Canada's resources, even if substantially expanded, could not have any significant impact if they were spread over a very large number of developing countries '.[15] It is, however, an objective not easily achieved; as Canada's aid appropriations increase, political pressure also grows to develop major programmes in an increasing number of countries; thus, while Nigeria and Ghana are the two countries of concentration in Commonwealth Africa, Tanzania, in 1971, was actually receiving more assistance than Ghana, and Indonesia has recently been added to the Asian list. CIDA has decided to try to preserve administrative flexibility by not revealing the list of countries of concentration, but it is already evident that this policy will be almost impossible to apply effectively.

Canadian foreign assistance began with the Colombo Plan in 1950 and at that time was devoted entirely to Commonwealth Asia. India and Pakistan have remained ever since areas of intense concentration. Although Canadian aid activity in the Pacific is now expanding, it is modest in all other countries of the region except Malaysia. With the attainment of independence by Commonwealth African states, Canada became an important donor in Ghana, Nigeria, and Tanzania. In recent

[14] *FPC: International Development*, pp. 18, 19.
[15] SCEAND, *3rd Report*, 4 June 1971.

years, for the reasons explained in Chapter 4, francophone Africa has also become an area of special interest, with the main effort in Tunisia, Cameroon, and Senegal. As a result, Canadian aid to Africa is now running at over $60 million annually. The Caribbean has also been an area of special Canadian effort ever since the support originally extended to the West Indies Federation. By contrast, assistance to Latin America is relatively small. Since 1964 some tied aid has been made available through the Inter-American Development Bank and small bilateral programmes were started in 1970 in four carefully selected South American areas.

The government has recently offered for the first time international assistance in birth-control. For Canada, whose population is 46 per cent Roman Catholic, this has been a controversial step. Indeed, the government was unable to compose differences and work out a policy in time for its inclusion in *Foreign Policy for Canadians*. The announcement, finally made in September 1970, linked limited support for voluntary agencies active in the field of birth-control in Canada with a modest international programme of assistance to countries which ask for it.

An important Canadian innovation in this field has been the establishment of the International Development Research Centre. This is a unique governmental institution, funded generously by the Canadian government ($30 million for its first five years of operation) with a board of directors of whom ten out of twenty-one are foreign nationals. Its approach is modelled on activities carried out by the Ford and Rockefeller Foundations, whose sponsored research has already contributed markedly to the 'green revolution'. The first director, Dr David Hopper, who has worked in the Philippines and India for both these foundations, has deliberately placed the entire emphasis of the Centre's research on work done in and with the full participation of developing countries.

Unlike the United States, Canadian public support for development assistance is remarkably strong. In spite of high levels of unemployment and major regional economic disparities, there is widespread advocacy of increased effort. All Canadian political parties support a substantial foreign-assistance programme, and the major opposition parties criticize the government for not doing enough. The unanimous report of the House committee[16] urged that the government strive to reach the 0·7 per cent target by 1975 and advanced a wide range of specific proposals for rendering Canadian foreign assistance more effective. The committee pressed for a comprehensive approach to development co-operation, placed major emphasis on the need for change in trade policy, and suggested ways of assuring that Canadian private investment is of genuine benefit to developing countries.

The Canadian Labour Congress, the major labour body of the country, has, since the early 1950s, favoured a Canadian commitment to the 1 per cent target. The Canadian Chamber of Commerce takes a similar position. There are approximately 150 voluntary agencies working in the foreign aid field and the Canadian University Service Overseas[17] has 1,100 volunteers abroad. The churches have increasingly become involved in development work, and they account for about 50 per cent of Canadians serving in developing countries, as compared to only 17 per cent who are supported by the government.

The Canadian idealist inclination in international affairs now seeks its primary outlet in international development assistance. The government senses the continuing public appeal of foreign aid and appears convinced that it is a role well-suited to Canada's concerns and capabilities. Professor Louis Sabourin has observed: ' Bien que le régime Trudeau ait une allure beaucoup plus " réaliste " que le régime Pearson, il faut reconnaître que, dans le domaine de l'assistance aux pays en voie de développement, l'esprit idéaliste demeure . . . le fondement de la politique de coopération internationale du Canada '.[18] There is every indication that developing countries will continue to turn to Canada and that the Trudeau government will respond with a quiet determination steadily to raise the priority given to activities in this field.

On this basis, Canada's relative aid performance among the

[16] There are remarkable parallels with the report of the UK Select Committee on Overseas Aid which was prepared during the same period, and which reached Canadian hands after the Standing Committee's report had been tabled.

[17] Equivalent to the British Volunteer Programme.

[18] ' L'Influence des facteurs internes sur la politique étrangère canadienne ', *Etudes internationales,* June 1970, p. 48.

industrialized countries will continue to climb. Development professionals hope that this quantitative growth will be matched by Canadian innovation in broadening and deepening the concept of development co-operation. There is also some hope that in concert with the growing efforts of other middle-ranking donors (e.g. the Scandinavians, Australia, and the Netherlands), the Canadian example may help to end the ' weariness of well-doing ' which has afflicted the major donors.

Canadians in the development field, however, like others all over the world, are troubled about the adequacy and, at times, the basic value of their efforts. This has led in many agencies to a perceptible shift to a new activism and a greater concentration on the home front—to inform and arouse their compatriots about the causes and consequences of world poverty. For it has become increasingly apparent that an effective national programme requires public knowledge and understanding. In the short term an appeal to the idealistic impulse of Canadians will suffice. But in the field of foreign assistance, where progress may be imperceptible, where conspicuous failures may be unavoidable and success hard to demonstrate, public support may crumble as it has in other countries. This would not only be a setback to world development activities. It could also leave Canadians without a satisfying and useful mode of international self-expression.

9

INDEPENDENCE THROUGH INTERNATIONALISM

THE FIRST and overriding objective of any state is national survival. In an age of continentalism, voluntary federation may begin to undermine the pre-eminence of this doctrine. But, this phenomenon excepted, the integrity of the state must be by definition the first test of any policy. Traditionally, the principal threat to national survival has been external aggression, and the effort to achieve military security—which can lead to highly aggressive behaviour—has therefore normally been the prime policy objective of the nation state.

Although freed from traditional security concerns by the unavoidable commitment of the United States to the defence of the whole of North America, Canada is, none the less, vitally concerned about its unity and integrity, challenged from within and from without. ' Canada is now plainly a country whose future is in question ', observed the London *Times* of 22 February 1971 in a special issue on Canada, referring particularly to the internal ' crisis of nationhood ' brought on by Quebec's revolutionary separatists late in 1970. At the same time the recurrent Canadian concern over being engulfed by the United States is at a high point. Both situations are dynamic. Both raise issues which are more domestic than foreign. Neither can be controlled by Ottawa, although policies—domestic and foreign —pursued by the Canadian government can aggravate or moderate these twin threats.

Canada had the unusual misfortune of achieving remarkable success almost from the moment of first appearing on the international stage—after World War II. Like a pop singer who strikes it rich without experiencing anonymity and having to struggle to survive, many Canadians came to believe that their country was uniquely qualified to mediate the world's problems and to act as the planet's conscience. As long as Canadian international activity was achieving dramatic successes, the

143

results spoke for themselves. But with the end of the exceptional postwar conditions and the consequent drying up of remarkable attainments, politicians began to try to substitute artful pretence for that which had formerly come naturally. Yet this only further aroused already exaggerated public expectations, and so compounded the politician's problem.

The first secretary of state for external affairs to face this public pressure was Howard Green, a man sensitive to popular feelings, but with no experience in foreign affairs. Taking office in 1958, within a year of Lester Pearson's Nobel peace prize for the triumph of UNEF, Green encouraged a practice of deliberately searching for ' initiatives ', most of all in the UN, so that Canada could be seen to be giving a lead to the world. Characteristic of the kind of policy which this approach led to was a resolution introduced by Canada at the 16th General Assembly, and subsequently approved, calling for the establishment of an international programme for measuring radioactive fall-out from nuclear explosions. Although the general support of the resolution could be displayed before the Canadian public as proof of Canada's wise leadership, the truth is that the requirements for furnishing readings of radiation levels would, had they ever been put fully into effect, have clogged the entire world's communication facilities. The resolution was observed, therefore, in the breach, and in the process both Canada's international reputation and the standing of the UN suffered among those who knew what was happening.

The Canadian public were not easily impressed by these rather procedural successes, and criticism of the country's foreign policy began to mount. Paul Martin took over as foreign minister in 1963 when this sense of frustration was becoming widespread. Martin, runner-up for the Liberal party leadership in 1957, believed that Pearson owed his convention victory to his Nobel prize. Hoping to succeed Pearson as prime minister when he retired, Martin could be excused for feeling that international achievements would help him in his goal. So he attempted to overcome public frustration by a desperate search for new successes in traditional areas of policy, an approach which he executed with tactical brilliance, but without having the good fortune of achieving any spectacular results. A prime example of this kind of diplomacy was the two missions of Chester Ronning, a retired Canadian diplomat with important personal contacts in China, to North Vietnam. Even when Martin gained success—for example, he played an important part in the Brussels meeting of NATO foreign ministers in 1966 which provided a device for France remaining within NATO—the Canadian idealistic strain was not impressed with the achievements. So Martin had increasingly to puff up Canada's accomplishments with words and procedural devices. In the process he only increased the scepticism felt in Canada about the nation's foreign policy.

The search for new roles

In a stimulating comparison of *Foreign Policy for Canadians* and President Nixon's *US Foreign Policy for the 1970s* [1] Dr Robert Osgood, who had been on the White House staff while the latter document was being prepared, noted that Canada's lack of the ' same kind of security interest ' as the United States meant:

that there is a less clear and widely shared standard in terms of priority of goals in Canada than in the United States . . . and hence it is natural that there is relatively more effort spent [in Canada] and in the Canadian [policy] paper on a kind of intellectual hand-wringing about abstract interests and principles, about such matters as interests versus roles, priorities among interests and that sort of thing. [2]

Canada's problem, in Osgood's judgement, is that, being prosperous and lacking ' security considerations . . . [which] clarify goals ', it suffers from being a dilettante in world affairs. Since Canadians have never had to defend the homeland against invasion and have lived for a century in isolation from the world's great terrors of war, pestilence, and famine, it is wholly natural that their view of the world should be altruistic. The object of foreign activity in their eyes is the promotion of international well-being. Professor Stephen Clarkson used this argument in 1969 to attack what he regarded as Canada's over-involvement in Europe:

[1] A report by President Nixon to the Congress, 25 Feb. 1970.
[2] SCEAND, *Mins of Proc. & Evidence*, 24 Feb. 1971, pp. 8, 9.

If the long term international aspirations of Canada are defined by where the needs are greatest, Europe now fully recovered from World War II must cede priority to the third world whose economic development is a moral as well as economic and political necessity.[3]

The strength of the idealist impulse in Canada has led governments in the past to stress altruistic motives for policies, thereby reinforcing public attitudes. Even where policies have directly promoted national interests, Canadians have not seen their actions in these terms. During the late 1940s and 1950s, when Canada was actively involved in building NATO and assisting to the limit of its means the economic rebuilding of Europe, the effort was regarded generally as activity undertaken because it was doing good for the Europeans. That the rebuilt economies of Europe would become important markets for Canadian products was not generally seen. There was, it is true, an awareness of the security threat posed by the Soviet Union, but the effort was justified as a defence of the democratic way of life, not a hard-headed pursuit of security—which is why the membership of Greece and Portugal in NATO comes in for criticism in Canada. This idealistic approach also explains the strong reaction of many Canadians, now that the European economies have been rebuilt, to what they regard as self-centred and selfish efforts to retain Canadian forces in Europe.

During this time, which coincides with Pearson's period as foreign minister, there was a close, although largely fortuitous coincidence between policies prompted by national interest and by idealism. The implications of this situation have scarcely been analysed by Canadian commentators. Garth Stevenson, in a fundamental criticism of the external policies of the Trudeau government, observed in passing that ' in the postwar period . . . the pragmatic tendency in Canadian foreign policy was supplemented and largely obscured, although not replaced, by the altruistic tendency '.[4] But his thesis was that Canadian policy should be essentially idealist, uncorrupted by the pragmatic pursuit of national interest.

For the reason noted by Professor Stevenson, the era during which Lester Pearson was minister for external affairs (1948–57)

---

[3] Ibid., 6 Mar. 1969, p. 1187.
[4] *For a Real Review* (Ottawa, Carleton Univ. Occasional papers, [1970]), p. 10.

was a period of national consensus in foreign policy. But for the detachment of French Canadians, very few of whom had at that time developed any interest in external affairs, the national consensus was almost as complete—although certainly not as intense—as was Britain's concentration under Churchill on the defeat of Nazi Germany. The American challenge loomed less large on the horizon, and was in any case largely eclipsed by the widely perceived dimensions of the Soviet threat. The internal challenge was in a period of dormancy: politically conscious French Canadians were preoccupied with the need to modernize the provincial institutions of Quebec, and French Canadians generally took pride in the fact that a compatriot, Louis St Laurent, was prime minister.

The situation has changed vastly during the last decade, both abroad and in Canada, and the Trudeau government has faced the need for a national stocktaking. This has involved the deliberate adoption of a more modest role in the world. The extent of the about turn in Canada's posture, which had under Paul Martin been that of a back-seat driver in international affairs, owes much to Trudeau's special kind of modesty, so surprisingly revealed in an airborne interview which took place during the return flight from Leningrad.

I'm a bit surprised at the tone in which [the Soviet leaders] are willing to deal with us as a great power . . . I kept saying no, you know we're a modest power; we're not going to try and pretend we're dealing with you as being a major power. You know my usual line, that Canada has over-extended itself in the postwar years in external policy and we're now more interested in what is good for Canada, not in making external policy. . . . We're not, in other words, trying to determine external events; we're just trying to make sure that our foreign policy helps our national policy.[5]

Foreign Policy for Canadians was intended to restore a sense of direction to and national confidence in Canadian foreign policy. This is a formidable task, and the government has only been partially successful. It has done important work in restoring a sense of proportion to Canada's international efforts; instead of trumpeting the country's importance in the world

[5] Office of PM, transcript of interview en route from Leningrad to Ottawa, 28 May 1971.

and then having to demonstrate in the UN, NATO, and elsewhere how much weight Canada carries in these bodies, the emphasis is now given to practical moves of direct interest to Canada, such as the recognition of the Chinese People's Republic and the development of practical co-operation with the USSR. Internationally these are both areas in which Canada is regarded as having achieved notable recent successes. The government too has so skilfully modified specific policies, such as the level of forces in Europe, as to win over most critics without generating new sources of opposition. One measure of accomplishment is the state of public interest. When Trudeau took office in 1968 he felt foreign policy to be sufficiently controversial to make it the subject of his first major policy statement. In 1971 public interest ranged from broad if rather passive support to indifference, and only relations with the United States continued to arouse strong feelings in many quarters.

Foreign Policy for Canadians has attracted more criticism for its omission, notably for its failure to deal substantially with relations with the United States, than for what it says. At a time of public preoccupation with this issue, it is hardly surprising that the informed public should have felt that the foreign-policy review was conspicuously incomplete. In spite of the monumental dimensions of the task of putting together the major elements of a Canadian policy for dealing with the United States, the government must accept that it cannot expect general support until Canadians can judge for themselves how it proposes to handle the problems.

The truth is that the government has not decided generally how to treat the United States. It has apparently worked out an approach to the complex problem of coping with US investment in Canada. It has produced a policy which was spectacularly successful in reassuring the Canadians that the Arctic would remain in Canadian hands. But what makes policy in this whole area so particularly difficult to elaborate is that, in addition to the intrinsic complexity of the problems themselves, policy must also—if it is to be effective—satisfy the emotional concerns of the public. Professor Hedley Bull of the Australian National University illuminated this subject while drawing some perceptive distinctions between problems which Canadian and Australian governments face in dealing with the United States.

The second major difference . . . is that Canada has a great problem of national identity. Canadians, as I understand it, are constantly asking themselves the question who they are. They are constantly in need of demonstrating to themselves and others how they differ from the United States. This appears to me to be something which gives Canadian policymakers an interest, having this psychological origin, in striking attitudes which are different from those of the United States, for their own sake. This is not an element in Australian policy.[6]

Bull had earlier noted that Canadians, unlike Australians, had the assurance that in terms of US security ' they will never be dispensable ', so that Canada has enjoyed a certain freedom to criticize the United States. ' Canadians feel they can cock a snook at the United States and be a thorn in her flesh without this having repercussions upon the willingness of the United States to come to Canada's defence '.

These observations go to the root of the problem. If one compares relations between Finland and the USSR on the one hand and Canada and the United States on the other, certain important differences stand out. Finns have no trouble identifying themselves, which is fortunate because the Russians would not tolerate the kind of criticism which Canadians direct at the United States, partly out of this need to distinguish themselves from their neighbours. For the same reason Canadians could not accept the kind of limitations on their freedom of action and even on their freedom to comment which Finns accept as the price of independence. Without wishing to push the parallel too far, it does illustrate the remarkable character of the Canada-United States relationship. From the Canadian government's point of view the constant question is how to balance the close co-operation which Canadians want and need with the United States, with the pursuit of policies which are recognizably different. For many Canadians, particularly among the more articulate section of the population, this requires taking a strong, independent stand. In an editorial in

[6] Standing Senate Cttee on For. Aff., *Proc.*, 8 Dec. 1970, p. 9.

the August 1971 issue of *Maclean's*, which describes itself as
Canada's national magazine, the editor (Peter Newman)
wrote:

It is, after all, our external contacts that help define the image of
ourselves, and if that image is always to be weak and accommodat-
ing, and if we can never find some independent way to express our
view of the world, then we have little future as an independent
country.

The widespread existence of this kind of sentiment presents
tremendous challenges to the Canadian policy-maker. For not
only must he calculate the national interest and devise a policy
to promote it; he must also take into account how the policy
will be viewed through this prism, which is the psychological
hang-up of Canadians toward the United States. This means
that great attention has to be given to the timing and the
presentation of decisions, to ensure that the impression is not
conveyed that Canada has been influenced in reaching them by
US pressure.

This difficult situation also explains the importance of
distinctive policies such as the recognition of the Chinese
People's Republic. The Trudeau government has shown itself
to be highly conscious of the possibilities of this approach, and
the international environment is propitious for the broadening
of contacts with all the communist states. As the Prime Minister
explained en route to Canada from his recent visit to the
USSR: ' Essentially what we are trying to do is to provide one
more instrument for the assurance to Canadians that they can
follow as independent a policy as possible. It shouldn't be
designed as anti-American or even as a counterbalance only to
the Americans '.[7] While the disclaimer in the last sentence was
justified because the reporter had asked whether an Arctic axis
was in the making, Canadian policy must seek counterweights
to balance the over-hanging power of the United States.

Although the present government's successes with China and
the USSR have provided some dramatic implementation of
this general policy, it has yet to make a concerted approach
towards Western Europe, where practical opportunities for

[7] Office of PM, transcript of interview with radio reporters en route from the
Soviet Union, 28 May 1971.

counterbalancing the United States are much more extensive. To date, tension with France has effectively ruled out any visits by the prime minister to continental Western Europe, and only a visit by Trudeau could give symbolic importance to a concerted approach to the new Europe. But even at the working level the government has not yet decided to make that commitment of resources and energy which would be needed to give substance to a broad approach to Europe. This hesitancy derives from continuing uncertainty as to how Canada should respond to the enlargement of the EEC. Until Canadian policy towards Europe is given clear objectives and dramatized by a prime ministerial visit to the continent, the policy of counterbalances can only be of limited effectiveness.

The need for a transcendent goal

If the government has been successful in clearing away some of the deficiencies of the past, it has been less effective in giving Canadians a new sense of purpose in the world. The emphasis placed in *Foreign Policy for Canadians* on the need to promote national objectives, so foreign to the way Canadians look on international activity, has aroused more criticism than support. The tone strikes one as being selfish, and in fact quite out of character with the actual policies which the government has pursued.

The policy papers have undoubtedly exaggerated the importance of promoting the national interest because politicians and professional diplomats alike felt that Canadian policy had increasingly lost touch with reality and was no longer serving national purposes. But this over-rational approach failed to take account of the very important principle expressed by Dr Osgood before the Commons Committee on External Affairs and National Defence:

You might think of the interests of a nation or the goals of a nation as being of two kinds: one self-interested and one transcendent. . . . The transcendent goals are not necessarily in conflict with these goals of self-interest. They add inspiration and drive but they are most compelling when they coincide somehow with the goals of self-interest.[8]

[8] As n. 2, p. 14: 7.

This need for an altruistic quality in foreign policy seems to be common to all peoples, but more strongly felt by Canadians than by most other peoples. The Trudeau government has yet to find—or perhaps, more correctly, to commit itself to policies, as did Pearson with such conspicuous success while he was foreign minister, which advance national interests and yet which can equally be presented in altruistic terms.

Foreign aid could provide a highly appropriate field for such treatment. No one challenges the importance of international development. Foreign aid has, moreover, the merit of offering an outlet for English-speaking and French-speaking Canadians alike, and it is a field in which the United States is no longer a world leader, so that concentration on such a policy could meet the key test of promoting both unity and independence. But to date, while significantly increasing the annual appropriations, Canada has declined to adopt a long-term commitment and to make the consequent financial undertakings for the future. Yet unless it does so, the government will fail to give to this activity a transcendent character which could provide a ' transforming, elevating and voluntarist tone [to] Canadian foreign policy '.[9]

The current concerns

The announcement in April 1969 of the government's decision to reduce Canadian forces in Europe gave rise to fears in Canada and abroad that Canada was set on an isolationist course. That the announcement was intended primarily to convey to Canadians the magnitude of the policy changes which the government was introducing rather than to reassure Europeans that Canada remained committed to Europe intensified the alarm felt abroad. These fears have surely now been stilled. *The Times* special issue of 22 February 1971 noted ' that, despite the challenge at home, this withdrawal from the outside world has reached its limit '.

There is another risk, however, that the modesty of the Trudeau government may lead it to underestimate Canada's actual capacity for effective action in the world. The prime minister's reference to Canada as a ' smaller power ', and even

[9] Hertzman & others, p. 133.

more his remarks while returning from Russia to the effect that ' we're more interested in what is good for Canada, . . . we're not . . . trying to determine external events ' reveal a scepticism about Canada's capacity to influence its external environment which might inhibit the government from undertaking useful international activity even where need, capability, and opportunity might coincide. It is significant, and troubling to some Canadians, that the Trudeau government never speaks in terms such as those suggested by Dr Osgood in his impressive appearance before the Commons Committee in February 1971:

I think it follows that the primary standard of choosing one policy as opposed to another is not what serves Candian security so much as whether the policy is in accord with your world responsibilities; whether it is the most effective use of available power; whether it is congruent with your dignity and independence, and with [your] internal cohesion and your economic welfare.[10]

This is the way the Canadian government used to speak when, under Lester Pearson as foreign minister, the country was making a major international contribution. Granted that Canadian power has declined relatively and that the rhetoric was somewhat corrupted in recent years; nevertheless the points made by Dr Osgood are still valid.

John Holmes, one of those concerned that the prime minister may ' think small ', had written in an essay published in 1965, before Trudeau had even entered politics, that ' the danger of delusions of grandeur is, on the whole, to be feared less than the danger of paralyzing abnegation '.[11] These things having been stated, however, the concern is for the future. For to date, when opportunities have arisen for useful action abroad, such as during the period leading up to the Commonwealth Conference in Singapore, the government has acted with intelligence and vigour. And since actions speak louder than words, it may be that there is no ground for concern.

The government has certainly made every effort to stimulate debate. The unusual first booklet of *Foreign Policy for Canadians*, in which the rationale for foreign policy is set out with surprising candour, is regarded by some former Canadian statesmen with

[10] As n. 2, p. 14: 9.
[11] *The Better Part of Valour* (1970), p. 27.

great experience as an error, producing no benefits and exposing the government to needless criticism. Yet in the face of the doubt and uncertainty felt by Canadians at this time in the country's future role, public debate is surely necessary.

If Canadians are to find their way out of their present predicament, they must understand themselves and, in this process, the detached foreign observer may be helpful in bringing the Canadian situation into perspective. For the country faces major problems, problems which affect both its integrity and its capacity for effective international action. There is no risk of a retreat into isolationism, as some had feared, because Canada needs to express its separate identity through international action. Big as the country is, it must seek external contacts to relieve it of the overwhelming presence of the United States. But until the immediate threat to the unity of the country is reduced, *The Times* is correct in concluding that the uncertainty of its future ' cannot but affect its authority and standing in the world community '. If some new modus vivendi can be found, the confidence engendered should of itself do much to restore a sense of purpose to Canadian foreign policy, by removing the doubts and preoccupations of the present. If the modus vivendi should include new concepts for integrating federal and provincial authorities in the process of developing foreign policy—which may well be necessary if the country is to survive—then Canada will indeed have made a contribution of importance to a world moving towards regional integration greater than anything devised during the days of high achievement under Lester Pearson.

BIBLIOGRAPHY

Canada, Dept of External Affairs. *Foreign policy for Canadians* (6 booklets). Ottawa, Queen's Printer, 1970.
—— White Paper, *Federalism and international relations.* Ottawa, Queen's Printer, 1968.
—— White Paper, *Federalism and international conferences on education.* Ottawa, Queen's Printer, 1971.
—— Dept. of National Defence. White Paper, *Defence in the 70s.* Ottawa, Queen's Printer, 1971.
Canadian Inst. Internat. Aff. *Canada in world affairs.* Biennial ser., vols. i-xii. Toronto, OUP.
Clarkson, S. ed. *An independent foreign policy for Canada?* Toronto/Montreal, McClelland & Stewart, 1968.
Creighton, D. G. *Canada's first century.* Toronto, Macmillan, 1970.
Crepeau, P. A. & C. B. MacPherson, eds. *The future of Canadian federalism/L'Avenir du federalisme canadien.* Univ. of Toronto Press/Presses de l'Université de Montréal, 1965.
Dickey, J. S. ed. *The United States and Canada.* Englewood Cliffs, Prentice Hall, 1964. (Esp. Eayrs, J., ' Sharing a continent, the hard issues ' and Holmes, J., ' The relationship in alliance and in world affairs '.)
Eayrs, J. *The art of the possible.* Univ. of Toronto Press, 1961.
Glazebrook, G. P. deT. *A history of Canadian external relations.* Toronto, Oxford University Press, 1950.
Gordon, J. King, ed. *Canada's role as a middle power.* Toronto, CIIA (printed and bound by J. Deyell, Lindsay, Ontario), 1966.
Gordon, W. L. *A choice for Canada, independence or colonial status.* Toronto, McClelland & Stewart, 1966.
Granatstein, J. L. *Canadian foreign policy since 1945: middle power or satellite?* Toronto, Copp Clark, 1969.
Hertzmann, L. & others. *Alliances and illusions—Canada and the NATO-NORAD question.* Edmonton, Hurtig, 1969.
Holmes, J. *The better part of valour: essays on Canadian diplomacy.* Toronto/Montreal, McClelland & Stewart, 1970.
International Journal, special issue, Winter 1970–1: *Canada's foreign policy.*
Levitt, K. *Silent surrender, the multinational corporation in Canada.* Toronto, Macmillan, 1970.
McLin, J. B. *Canada's changing defence policy, 1957–63.* Toronto, Copp Clark, 1967.

Merchant, L. & A. D. P. Heeney. ' Canada and the United States, principles for partnership ', *Department of State Bulletin*, 2 Aug. 1965.

Trudeau, P. E. *Federalism and the French Canadians.* Toronto, Macmillan, 1968.

INDEX

Accord cadre (Canada-France), 42
Africa (*see also* Francophone confer-
ences), 42–5, 98, 122–31, 139–40
l'Agence de Coopération culturelle et
technique, 43, 44, 45, 50
Agreements (*see also* NORAD; treaties),
25, 30, 32, 42, 52, 66, 75, 79, 80, 100,
120–1
Aid and development, 42, 43, 50, 97,
101, 108, 115, 117, 118, 120–1, 130,
134, 136–42, 152
Alaska oil pipeline, 74–5
Alberta, 38, 53
Allied Command Europe Mobile
Force, 36
Amchitka nuclear test, 33–4, 75
Anti-Submarine Warfare (ASW), 26
Arctic, 30, 61, 69–75, 76, 77, 148
Arctic Waters Pollution Prevention
Act, 71, 72, 77
Arms control (*see* disarmament)
Arms sales, 25, 80, 123–4, 128
Asia, 98, 103–15, 139
Asian Development Bank, 107
l'Association des parlementaires de
langue française, 50
l'Association des universités partielle-
ment et entièrement de langue
française (AUPELF), 50
Atomic Energy Commission, 31
Australia, 18, 109, 112–13
Automotive Agreement, Canada-US,
79, 81, 83

Balance-of-payments crisis: 1971, 31,
59, 83–5, 95, 99
Bangladesh, 114–15
Belgium, 42
Biafran conflict, 18, 115, 125–8
BOMARC bases, 37
Bilinguism and biculturalism, 40, 50,
66
Bourassa, Robert, 48
Brazil, 117–18
Brezhnev, Leonid, 29
Broadcasting, 40, 60, 66

Cabinet, 11, 12, 13, 14, 37, 50, 55, 64,
72, 127

Cadieux, Léo, 37, 55
Cambodia, 108
Canada Shipping Act, 71, 72
Canadian International Development
Agency (CIDA), 44, 136–9
Canadian Institute of International
Affairs (CIIA), 9
Canadian Labour Congress, 27, 65,
66, 141
Canadian Radio and Television Com-
mission (CRTC), 67
Canadian University Service Overseas
(CUSO), 129, 141
Canairelief, 128
Capital (*see* investment)
Caribbean, 51, 115, 117, 119–22, 130,
140
Ceylon, 18, 110
China, P. R. of, 3, 93, 103–7, 148, 150
Chrétien, Jean, 30
Churches, 15, 33, 125, 129, 141
Cold War, 1, 3, 23, 25, 146
Colombo Plan, 139
Commission on International Develop-
ment, 137
Committee for an Independent Canada,
63–4
Committee on the Challenges of
Modern Society, 100
Common Agricultural Policy (CAP),
92, 93
Common Market (*see* EEC)
Commonwealth, 2, 42, 43, 45, 98, 113,
114, 122–5, 130, 139
— conferences, 18, 109, 120–1, 123–5
Communications, 39, 40, 41, 59, 60,
66–7, 77, 125
Conference of the Committee on
Disarmament, 32
Conservative Party, 20, 28, 31
Constitutional issues (*see* federal-
provincial relations; Governor-
General)
Continental defence (*see* ASW;
NORAD)
Continental integration, 77–81, 86, 87,
143
Corporations, multinational (*see* foreign
ownership; investment)
Council of Europe, 100